THE POET'S COMPANION

POETRY BY KIM ADDONIZIO

The Philosopher's Club
Jimmy & Rita

POETRY BY DORIANNE LAUX

Awake
What We Carry

THE POET'S COMPANION

A Guide to the Pleasures of Writing Poetry

KIM ADDONIZIO AND
DORIANNE LAUX

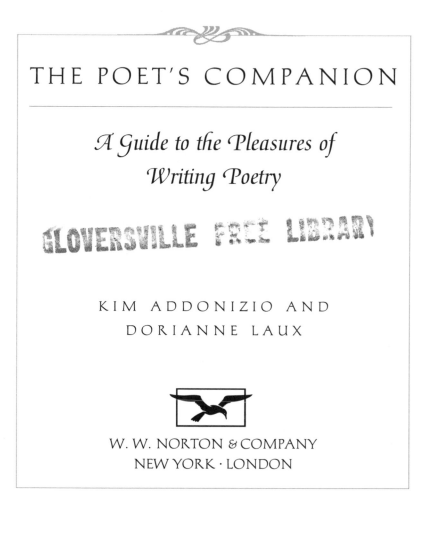

W. W. NORTON & COMPANY
NEW YORK · LONDON

The text of this book is composed in Electra
with the display set in Michelangelo and Medici Script
Composition by White River Publishing Services
Manufacturing by the Maple-Vail Book Manufacturers Group.
Book design by JAM DESIGN

Library of Congress Cataloging-in-Publication Data

Addonizio, Kim (date)
The poet's companion : a guide to the pleasures of writing poetry / Kim Addonizio and
Dorianne Laux.
p. cm.
Includes bibliographical references and index.
ISBN 0-393-31654-8

1. Poetry—Authorship. I. Laux, Dorianne. II. Title.
PN1042.A35 1997
808.1—dc21   96-40451
                                                                        CIP

W. W. Norton & Company, Inc., 500 Fifth Avenue, New York, N.Y. 10110
http://www.wwnorton.com

W. W. Norton & Company Ltd., 10 Coptic Street, London WC1A 1PU

1 2 3 4 5 6 7 8 9 0

For our daughters,
Tristem and Aya;
and for our students,
who continue to inspire us.

Contents

Acknowledgments

We wish to thank our editor, Carol Houck Smith, as well as Anna Karvellas and Fred Courtright, all of Norton, for their help in completing this project. Additional thanks to Villa Montalvo in Saratoga, California, for a residency which enabled us to work together on the book. We're also grateful to Scott Reid for all his helpful e-mails about the Internet. And to Amy Kossow, our wonderful agent, for her persistence and faith.

Introduction

This book grew out of our daily concerns as poets, and out of our work as teachers of poetry. For several years we offered one-day intensive workshops in the San Francisco Bay Area, exploring issues and ideas with all kinds of writers. Additionally, we've taught classes in prisons, community colleges, high schools, at writers' conferences, and in university creative writing programs. Our students have been wonderfully varied: carpenters, therapists, waiters, retired persons, housewives and househusbands, photographers, word processors, systems analysts—in short, a cross-section of our community. They've ranged from absolute beginners to publishing poets with graduate degrees. All of them have had one thing in common: the desire to write poetry, and to do it well.

We wanted to create a book that would focus on both craft and process. Craft provides the tools: knowing how to make a successful metaphor, when to break a line, how to revise and rewrite—these are some of the techniques the aspiring poet must master. And the study of craft is lifelong; the exercises offered here should be useful even for experienced poets who want to further hone their skills. Process, the day-to-day struggle to articulate experience, is equally important; so we've devoted a portion of this book to the writing process itself. Within these pages you'll find not only a guide to the nuts and bolts of how poems are made, but discussions ranging from how to tackle your subject to how to cope with rejection and self-doubt. We've also included practical information like how to submit your work for publication and what the Internet has to offer poets; and there's even a chapter on grammar, a subject too often neglected in creative writing classes.

This book can be used in a number of ways. In a semester-long class or workshop, each chapter in "Subjects for Writing" and "The Poet's Craft" might form the basis for the week's activities. "The Writing Life" can offer the student inspiration and information outside of class; further ideas for creating new poems are taken up in "Twenty-Minute Writing Exercises"—ideal when working with a group. If you're reading this book on your own, let it be your teacher, leading you towards new knowledge and enlivening your imagination. Get together with others, if possible, and assign yourselves weekly exercises from the book, and meet to share the results.

We think you'll find this an accessible guide to the pleasures of reading and writing poetry. The exercises we've developed have proven to be useful catalysts for the creation of new and interesting work, both for ourselves and our students. The poems we've chosen are ones we've loved and found to be important to our growth as poets and human beings. We've avoided including poems that are already widely available in many anthologies and textbooks, and we haven't included any of the fine world poetry available in translation; instead, this book focuses on contemporary poems by American writers, to introduce you to poetry as it is right now, with its concern for both timeless and timely subjects.

Of course, there's a rich and varied poetic tradition that we hope you are already acquainted with, or will be inspired to seek out. Poet Stanley Kunitz called the tradition of poetry "the sacred word"; the poetry being written in present times he characterized as the living word. Both are important to poets. It's crucial to read what's being written now, to see how the language is changing and evolving; new words enter it daily, while others fall into disuse or take on different meanings. It's important to speak, and listen, to a contemporary community of readers and writers. But it's equally crucial to see where the

language came from, how it was fashioned and refashioned by poets of the past. To write without any awareness of a tradition you are trying to become a part of would be self-defeating. Every artist alive responds to the history of his or her art—borrowing, stealing, rebelling against, and building on what other artists have done. This book is only a small part of the whole. Occasionally, our writing exercises suggest that you read a particular poem, but the poem is not included. We urge you to seek out those poems as models, and we encourage browsing through a particular book or anthology. The appendices to this book include further readings that will involve you more deeply with poems and poetic craft.

Most of all, we hope you'll continue to write, to read widely, and to support an art which offers profound rewards, though they're rarely material. Buy collections of poetry, go to readings, and meet others who feel a similar love of the word. In an age of consumerism and declining literacy, this is more than ever a necessity. William Carlos Williams wrote, "It is difficult to get the news from poems, but men die miserably every day for lack of what is found there." And we might add: women, too. We need more poets, not fewer, as some critics of creative writing programs would have it. We invite you to do what Russian novelist Leo Tolstoy asked: to add your light to the sum of light. Do it with patience, and love, and respect for the depth and difficulty of the task. This book is offered in that spirit.

THE POET'S COMPANION

SUBJECTS FOR WRITING

Writing and Knowing

We've been told again and again to write about what we know, but we don't trust that advice. We think our lives are dull, ordinary, boring. Other people have lives worthy of poetry, but not us. And what are the "great" poems about? The big subjects: death, desire, the nature of existence. They ask the big questions: Who are we? Why are we here? Where are we going? We find it difficult to believe those subjects, those questions, can be explored and contained in a poem about working at a fast food restaurant, a poem about our best friend, a poem about washing the dishes, tarring the roof, or taking a bus across town. If C. K. Williams had believed this, he might not have written "Tar," which is at one level a poem about fixing the roof, and at another, about the end of the world. Carolyn Forché might not have written "As Children Together," a poem about her best friend which is also about how we choose one life path over another. In the nineteenth century, John Keats wrote to a nightingale, an urn, a season. Simple, everyday things that he knew. Walt Whitman described the stars, a live oak, a field. Elizabeth Bishop wrote about catching a fish, Wallace Stevens about a Sunday morning, William Carlos Williams about a young housewife and a red wheelbarrow. They began with what they knew, what was at hand, what shimmered around them in the ordinary world. That's what Al Zolynas did in this poem:

THE ZEN OF HOUSEWORK

I look over my own shoulder
down my arms
to where they disappear under water
into hands inside pink rubber gloves
moiling among dinner dishes.

My hands lift a wine glass,
holding it by the stem and under the bowl.
It breaks the surface
like a chalice
rising from a medieval lake.

Full of the grey wine
of domesticity, the glass floats
to the level of my eyes.
Behind it, through the window
above the sink, the sun, among
a ceremony of sparrows and bare branches,
is setting in Western America.

I can see thousands of droplets
of steam—each a tiny spectrum—rising
from my goblet of grey wine.
They sway, changing directions
constantly—like a school of playful fish,
or like the sheer curtain
on the window to another world.

Ah, grey sacrament of the mundane!

This is where we begin, by looking over our own shoulder, down our own arms, into our own hands at what we are holding, what we know. Few of us begin to write a poem about "death" or "desire." In fact, most of us begin by either looking outward: that blue bowl, those shoes, these three white clouds. Or inward: I remember, I imagine, I wish, I wonder, I want.

Look at the beginnings of some of Emily Dickinson's poems: "There's a certain slant of light . . . " "A clock stopped . . . " "A bird came down the walk . . . " "I heard a fly buzz . . . " and these first words: "The flesh . . ." "The brain . . . " "The heart . . . " "The truth . . . " "A route . . . " "A word . . . " There is a world inside each of us that we know better than anything else, and a world outside of us that calls for our attention—the world of our families, our communities, our history. Our subject matter is always with us, right here, at the tips of our fingers, at the edge of each passing thought.

The trick is to find out what we know, challenge what we know, own what we know, and then give it away in language: I love my brother, I hate winter, I always lose my keys. You have to know and describe your brother so well he becomes everyone's brother, to evoke the hatred of winter so passionately that we all begin to feel the chill, to lose your keys so memorably we begin to connect that action to all our losses, to our desires, to our fears of death. Good writing works from a simple premise: your experience is not yours alone, but in some sense a metaphor for everyone's. Poems that fail to understand this are what a writer once parodied in a three-line illustration:

> Here I stand
> looking out my window
> and I am important.

Of course our lives are important, meaningful. But our daily experiences, our dreams and loves and passionate convictions about the world, won't be important to others—to potential readers of our poems—unless we're able to transform the raw material of our experiences into language that reaches beyond the self-involvement of that person standing at the window, so that what we know becomes shared knowledge, part of who we are as individuals, a culture, a species.

What do we all know? We know our lives. We all go through childhood, adolescence, adulthood and old age. We can write about it. Some of us go through marriage, childbirth, parenthood, divorce. We work, we go to school, we form bonds of friendship and love, we break dishes in anger, we daydream, we follow the news or turn from it in despair, we forget. These are all subjects for our poems, the moments in our own personal lives that need telling, that are worth our attention and preservation.

Poetry is an intimate act. It's about bringing forth something that's inside you—whether it is a memory, a philosophical idea, a deep love for another person or for the world, or an apprehension of the spiritual. It's about making something, in language, which can be transmitted to others—not as information, or polemic, but as irreducible art. Walt Whitman's "Song of Myself" begins, "I celebrate myself, and sing myself, / and what I assume you shall assume, / for every atom belonging to me as good belongs to you." Whitman died in 1892, but the spirit embodied in his language still speaks to us—passionate, intimate, inclusive.

Here's a poem by former Poet Laureate Rita Dove, about a moment between mother and daughter which comes out of everyday experience and startles us with its frank intimacy:

AFTER READING *MICKEY IN THE NIGHT KITCHEN*
FOR THE THIRD TIME BEFORE BED

I'm in the milk and the milk's in me! . . . I'm Mickey!

My daughter spreads her legs
to find her vagina:
hairless, this mistaken
bit of nomenclature
is what a stranger cannot touch
without her yelling. She demands
to see mine and momentarily
we're a lopsided star
among the spilled toys,
my prodigious scallops
exposed to her neat cameo.

And yet the same glazed
tunnel, layered sequences.
She is three; that makes this
innocent. *We're pink!*
she shrieks, and bounds off.

Every month she wants
to know where it hurts
and what the wrinkled string means
between my legs. *This is good blood*
I say, but that's wrong, too.
How to tell her that it's what makes us—
black mother, cream child.
That we're in the pink
and the pink's in us.

Dove's poem is about knowledge of the body; the body, after all, is the starting point for what we know. Whitman also wrote, "I sing the body electric," and poets from earliest times have been doing just that, celebrating its sensual pleasures, contemplating its desires and the limits of those desires. In modern and contemporary poetry, a number of writers have taken the body as their subject, with memorable results.

We begin with our selves. We are not only body, but heart and mind and imagination and spirit. We can talk about all those things, about what it is like to be alive at the end of the twentieth century. Wendell Berry has written about marriage, Galway Kinnell about the birth of his children, Sharon Olds about motherhood and pet funerals and her first boyfriend. These and other poets began with the simple idea that what they saw and experienced was important to record, and that the modest facts of their lives, what they knew within the small confines of their limited, personal worlds, could contain the enduring facts and truths of the larger world.

That much said, how about what we *don't* know? That's subject matter for our poems as well. Every good poem asks a question, and every good poet asks every question. No one can call herself a poet unless she questions her ideas, ethics, and beliefs. And no one can call himself a poet unless he allows the self to enter into the world of discovery and imagination. When we don't have direct experience to guide us, we always have our imagination as a bridge to knowledge. Here's a poem by Susan Mitchell that details what she can't know, but can imagine:

THE DEAD

At night the dead come down to the river to drink.
They unburden themselves of their fears,
their worries for us. They take out the old photographs.
They pat the lines in our hands and tell our futures,
which are cracked and yellow.
Some dead find their way to our houses.
They go up to the attics.
They read the letters they sent us, insatiable
for signs of their love.
They tell each other stories.
They make so much noise
they wake us
as they did when we were children and they stayed up
drinking all night in the kitchen.

The poet has mixed the ordinary with the fantastic to convince us that the dead, indeed, act this way. At the end of the poem, the dead merge with the memory of the living—parents or relatives who "stayed up / drinking all night in the kitchen." Death is a mystery for all of us, one of the many things we don't understand about the world; poets want and need to explore such mysteries. Poetry would be dull indeed if we limited ourselves only to the things we think we already comprehend; it would be limited, self-satisfied, the poem finished before it was even begun. Robert Frost said, "No surprise for the writer, no surprise for the reader."

But the old advice, "Write about what you know," is still an excellent place to begin. Start with that, and let yourself move out from what you know into the larger questions. If it worked for Whitman and Dickinson, for Williams and Forché and Dove, it can work for you. Here's what David Lee has to say about it in this prose poem from his first book:

LOADING A BOAR

We were loading a boar, a goddamn mean big sonofabitch and he jumped out of the pickup four times and tore out my stockracks and rooted me in the stomach and I fell down and he bit John on the knee and he thought it was broken and so did I and the boar stood over in the far corner of the pen and watched us and John and I just sat there tired and Jan laughed and brought us a beer and I said, "John it ain't worth it, nothing's going right and I'm feeling half dead and haven't wrote a poem in ages and I'm ready to quit it all," and John said, "shit young feller, you ain't got started yet and the reason's cause you trying to do it outside yourself and ain't looking in and if you wanna by god write pomes you gotta write pomes about what you know and not about the rest and you can write about pigs and that boar and Jan and you and me and the rest and there ain't no way you're gonna quit," and we drank beer and smoked, all three of us, and finally loaded that mean bastard and drove home and unloaded him and he bit me again and I went in the house and got out my paper and pencils and started writing and found out John he was right.

It certainly worked for Lee, author of *The Porcine Legacy* and *The Porcine Canticles*. He took John's advice to heart and wrote not just one poem, but books of poems about what he knew. And what he knew was pigs. You don't need to travel to exotic places or live through revolutions to write good poems. If you have a life full of drama, then of course that will be your material. But don't wait for something to happen before you begin to write; pay attention to the world around you, right now. That's what poets do. This is how Ellery Akers describes it:

WHAT I DO

I drive on country roads, where kangaroo rats shoot across the blacktop and leap into the bushes, where feral cats streak through fields, and cows lift their heads at the sound of the car but don't stop chewing, where the horses' manes blow in the wind and the cheat grass blows, and the grapes are strapped to stakes as if they have been crucified

I drive past the Soledad liquor store, where the neon starts, and the argon, past the *Ven-A-Mexico* restaurant, past the fields full of white hair—it's just water spurting across all that lettuce—and a jackrabbit runs and freezes, and the Digger Pines stand on either side of the road and the car plunges over the cattleguards, rattling—

Sometimes I listen to the earth, it has a sound: deep inside, the garnets
    churning

Sometimes I listen to the birds: the sharp *whir* in the air as the swallow veers over my head, as the wren flies, panting, carrying a twig longer than she is, and by this time I can tell by the sounds of their wings, without looking, whether a titmouse just passed—*flutter*—a raven—*thwack, thwack*—an eagle—*shud, shud, shud*—big wet sheets flapping on a laundry line

I paint: I draw: I swab gesso on canvas, stropping the brushes again and again, rinsing them, as the paler and paler tints go down the drain

I cook, I shell peas, breaking open the pods at the veins with a snap: I take vitamins—all the hard, football-shaped pills—sometimes they get stuck in my gullet and I panic and think what a modern way to die, they'll come and find my dead, perfectly healthy body

I pay attention to the willows: I sniff the river
I collect otoliths, and the small ear bones of seals
I notice the dead mouse on the path, its tail still curled, its snout eaten
    away by ants

So that although I've forgotten what John and I said to each other outside the airport, I remember the cedar waxwings chattering and lighting on the telephone wires, the clipped stiff grass and how sharp it was against my thighs as the waxwings flashed by

And when I teach, I explain about semicolons, the jab of the period, the curl of the comma: the two freights of verbs and subjects on either side like a train coupling

I pick up spiders in my house, sliding a cup over them and a piece of paper under them, toss them, and watch them sail out the window. I catch moths the same way, open the latch with one hand and watch them come back and bumble against the glass, wanting the light

Bather in the night, the soap slides next to me in the tub
Phone dialer when I'm scared, and want to hear Peter's voice, or Valerie's or Barbara's,
Xeroxer, the faint green light pulses over and over, repeating my name as my poems flick by, and the machine spits out copy after copy
Swimmer, slow breast stroke, hand over hand, kick

I stand at the lectern in my jacket, always a jacket to cover up my breasts so I don't feel so naked

I watch as the clouds shred slowly outside and inside, as the hummingbird sits in her deep cup, her bill sticking out, as the phalarope flies around me in circles in the saw-grass and spartina and she wants me to leave her alone so I leave her alone

I squelch through mud in my sneakers and watch Barbara garden and remember to eat her tomatoes:

I bait traps with bird-seed and the door springs shut and I grope for sparrows as they flutter frantically away and I reach into the far corner of the cage and gently clasp them and put them in my bird-bag tied to my belt, so as I walk the bag keeps banging at my hips: and then, at the observatory, I take one out, and blow on her skull, fasten a band around her leg, toss her out the window and let her go:

I listen to myself: this kind of listening is both tedious and courageous

Depression is part of it too: sometimes I bolt awake at night, feeling a man is pressing on top of me, certain it's happening

I see my therapist, my words fill up the room, the past is enormous, I steer towards anger and practice anger as if it were Italian, I throw stones at the canyon and yell and sometimes a clump of shale falls down and a spider races out

I watch tadpoles sink, and water striders: once, six miles in at Mud Lake, some drunken men, a rifle crack, I ran the whole way to the car—

I come back to Soledad: at night plume moths and geometrid moths flatten themselves against the motel windows, looking like chips of bark, and in the

morning a starling teeters across the trash bin—pecking at cellophane, walking over the styrofoam containers from McDonald's. A man who looks
scared says, "Good Morning, Ma'am," as he throws away more styrofoam,
and I drive under the cool overpass where pigeons nest every year, flapping
up into the steel slots, as the trucks go down with their loads—

Needing to pile up silence outside me and within me
the silence underneath the bulbs of Zygodene, Stink-horn and blood-red
    saprophytes—

as the minutes open into parachutes that fall and fall again

Akers has beautifully evoked the world of one poet. As the minutes
of your own life open and fall, catch them in poems. You've been
given one life, one set of unique experiences; out of those particulars,
make the poems only you can make.

IDEAS FOR WRITING

1. Make a list of the most memorable events in your life. Some of
   them will be large—a death, a breakup, some goal you finally
   accomplished. But list the small things, too, things you've always
   remembered as particularly special and important in some way.
   When you're finished, you should have a list of subjects for
   poems that could take you years to write. For now, start a poem
   about one of the events you've listed; every so often, you can go
   back to the list and pick another one.

2. List the objects in your bedroom or living room. Write a poem
   describing them and telling a little of their—and your—history.
   A good poem to read first is "Photograph of My Room" by
   Carolyn Forché, in her book The Country Between Us.

3. What do you do every day—or on a regular basis? Write a poem
   about showering, or jogging, or cooking, and so on. Try, in the
   poem, to get at the particular way you perform this activity, that
   might be different from someone else.

4. What are the things you love? The things you hate? List them in two columns. Now, write a poem that combines something you love with something you hate.

5. Begin a poem with the words, "I don't know . . ." You might list several things you don't know, or focus on a particular thing.

6. Begin a poem with a question word: Who, what, where, when, why, how. Ask a big question about life, and then try to answer it from your own experience. (A good poem which asks a lot of questions is "In a U-Haul North of Damascus" in the last section of this book.)

7. Write a poem instructing a reader how to do something you know how to do. First make a list of all the things you can do (hit a tennis ball, change a diaper, identify wildflowers, etc.). Remember that you don't want to sound like an instruction manual, but a poem; make it beautiful, make the lesson one that tells someone about how to live in the world.

The Family:
Inspiration and Obstacle

We've encouraged you to write about what you know, what you are close to; and nothing is closer to home than the family. But how do we write about this particularly personal group of people with the honesty and openness that is required of us as poets? The subject is one that all of us can "relate" to; we each come from some kind of family. Whether it be traditional or nontraditional, we all grow up with a constellation of others around us who shape and influence us, and that influence remains a part of our lives. It's through our relationships with our parents, siblings, cousins, grandparents that we first learn about the extremes of intimacy and distance, anger and joy, cruelty and kindness, isolation and community. The family is our first small look at the ways of the larger world. It is in this microcosm that we begin to see who we are, and how we fit in or don't.

Sometimes, writing about our families can be painful. Many of our students have expressed discomfort about exposing themselves and their families in their poems. This is a legitimate concern when it comes to publishing; you may want to do as others have done and write in the third person, or change significant details wherever possible, or write under a pseudonym. But what about the larger discomfort of exposing our vulnerabilities and revealing secrets? If you need permission, you can look to others who have written memorable poems about their families—Stanley Kunitz, Robert Lowell, Theodore Roethke, Sylvia Plath, and more recently just about everybody, but especially Sharon Olds. Louise Glück's *Ararat* dissects family relationships in starkly beautiful poems. In *Eva-Mary*, Linda McCarriston deals with sexual abuse and other issues. Julia Kasdorf's *Sleeping Preacher* explores her family's Mennonite roots, while Minnie Bruce Pratt's *Crimes Against Nature* details the struggles of a lesbian mother who loses her sons. Everyone deals with the issue of exposure in their own way, and you will have to find yours. The point is, don't let anything keep you from getting it down on the page. You can decide later whether to show it to anyone, whether to publish it in a journal or include it in a book. In the meantime, what you'll discover in your reading is that writing about the family is an American tradition, a way of knowing about ourselves.

Carolyn Forché has memorialized her grandmother, Anna, in a number of poems. This one begins her first book, *Gathering the Tribes*:

THE MORNING BAKING

Grandma come back, I forgot
How much lard for these rolls?

Think you can put yourself in the ground
Like plain potatoes and grow in Ohio?

I am damn sick of getting fat like you
Think you can lie through your Slovak?

Tell filthy stories about the blood sausage?
Pish-pish nights at the virgin in Detroit?

I blame your raising me up for my Slav tongue
You beat me up out back, taught me to dance

I'll tell you I don't remember any kind of bread
Your wavy loaves of flesh

Stink through my sleep
The stars on your silk robe

But I'm glad I'll look when I'm old
Like a gypsy dusha hauling milk

The first lines of the poem are a plea for the dead grandmother to return, and set us up for a poem of longing. But by the third line we begin to feel another tone creeping in, and later an anger that comes full force by the fifth line and continues for a few more. This is a poem that defies polite social standards in how it speaks about the old as well as the dead; old or dead relatives never lie, talk dirty, beat us. They don't hand down to us our worst traits. And if they stink and are overweight, we don't speak of it. But this narrator does, giving us the difficult facts. Yet this ultimately becomes a love poem. How? Look at the way Forché continues to set us up emotionally for one feeling and then surprises us with another: "You beat me up out back, taught me to dance . . . " "Your wavy loaves of flesh / Stink through my sleep / The stars on your silk robe . . . " Forché walks a fine line between rage and sorrow, repulsion and awe, embarrassment and tenderness, and she does that not by repressing the negative, but by including both sides of the emotional story. By the end of the poem we are struck with a sense of the narrator's deep ambivalence about her grandmother, reminding us of the truth of our own disquieting feelings about those close to us.

Tolstoy's great novel *Anna Karenina* opens with these lines: "All happy families are like one another; each unhappy family is unhappy in its own way." We have sometimes heard the complaint from students that they have nothing to write about because they have not suffered enough. Not all of us have endured a childhood filled with grief and trauma, and to wish for one seems a bit far to go in the service of your art. Besides, such a childhood doesn't guarantee you'll have the ability to make poetry of it, though it might well be part of the reason you'd want to write. We've been startled by how often some early loss or trauma appears in the work of writers and other artists: a parent's suicide, a sibling's death, an abusive parent or family friend. Such early wounds stay with us, and may become sources or obsessions in later creative work. But there's no equation between good poetry and unhappy families. We each write out of our own constellation of experiences. Writing about trauma can be a good way of coming to terms with it; making it into poetry is another thing. But no matter what your background, one thing is certain: our formative years are rife with material for poetry. They are a time of learning and discovery, a generous landscape of memory and insight. Let's look at a poem by Li-Young Lee that focuses on an early childhood experience.

THE GIFT

To pull the metal splinter from my palm
my father recited a story in a low voice.
I watched his lovely face and not the blade.
Before the story ended, he'd removed
the iron sliver I thought I'd die from.

I can't remember the tale,
but hear his voice still, a well
of dark water, a prayer.
And I recall his hands,
two measures of tenderness
he laid against my face,
the flames of discipline
he raised above my head.

Had you entered that afternoon
you would have thought you saw a man
planting something in a boy's palm,
a silver tear, a tiny flame.
Had you followed that boy
you would have arrived here,
where I bend over my wife's right hand.

Look how I shave her thumbnail down
so carefully she feels no pain.
Watch as I lift the splinter out.
I was seven when my father
took my hand like this,
and I did not hold that shard
between my fingers and think,
Metal that will bury me,
christen it Little Assassin,
Ore Going Deep for My Heart.
And I did not lift up my wound and cry,

Death visited here!
I did what a child does
when he's given something to keep.
I kissed my father.

This is a tender poem that skirts the edge of sentimentality and yet never slips over that edge into bathos. But how is it done? Let's go back to the opening line and see how we are directed by it. "My father recited a story in a low voice." How many childhood stories begin this way, in a patient, wise, and almost conspiratorial voice that invites the child in? Lee sets us up to listen by mimicking that voice. Then he tells us his story in much the same way we imagine his father told him stories as a child, simply, directly, with a bit of overt drama or exaggeration here and there to get the really important points across: "the iron sliver I thought I'd die from . . . " reminding us of the kind of inflated language a child might use to describe pain. He also employs the use of fairy tale imagery: "a silver tear, a tiny flame . . . " and "Metal that will bury me . . . " and later, even a touch of the Shakespearean: "*Death visited here!*" It's as if the author anticipates our world-weary cynicism and doubt and then pulls us in, like children, with a good story. Lee also uses some of the same techniques Forché has used in her grandmother poem: pushing contradictory emotions up against each other to achieve a feeling of believability: ". . . his hands, / two measures of tenderness / he laid against my face, / the flames of discipline / he raised above my head." But it is the story that continues to draw us in and hold the poem together. And the poem is larger than its parts, becoming a story about how parents pass on the qualities of love, tenderness, and endurance to their offspring, the small but important gifts we give to one another.

Sisters or brothers, especially those close in age, grow up beside each other, know each other in a way no one else ever will. In this poem by Philip Levine, the brother becomes larger and more symbolic as the poem progresses; by looking closely at the brother, the poet is able to look at himself, and at the difficulties and limitations of the larger world.

YOU CAN HAVE IT

My brother comes home from work
and climbs the stairs to our room.
I can hear the bed groan and his shoes drop
one by one. You can have it, he says.

The moonlight streams in the window
and his unshaven face is whitened
like the face of the moon. He will sleep
long after noon and waken to find me gone.

Thirty years will pass before I remember
that moment when suddenly I knew each man
has one brother who dies when he sleeps
and sleeps when he rises to face this life,

and that together they are only one man
sharing a heart that always labors, hands
yellowed and cracked, a mouth that gasps
for breath and asks, Am I gonna make it?

All night at the ice plant he had fed
the chute its silvery blocks, and then I
stacked cases of orange soda for the children
of Kentucky, one gray boxcar at a time

with always two more waiting. We were twenty
for such a short time and always in
the wrong clothes, crusted with dirt
and sweat. I think now we were never twenty.

In 1948 in the city of Detroit, founded
by de la Mothe Cadillac for the distant purposes
of Henry Ford, no one wakened or died,
no one walked the streets or stoked a furnace,

for there was no such year, and now
that year has fallen off all the old newspapers,
calendars, doctors' appointments, bonds,
wedding certificates, drivers licenses.

The city slept. The snow turned to ice.
The ice to standing pools or rivers
racing in the gutters. Then bright grass rose
between the thousands of cracked squares,

and that grass died. I give you back 1948.
I give you all the years from then
to the coming one. Give me back the moon
with its frail light falling across a face.

Give me back my young brother, hard
and furious, with wide shoulders and a curse
for God and burning eyes that look upon
all creation and say, You can have it.

Levine's image of the shared heart of brothers is beautiful and apt;
a sibling can be a mirror, a path to memory. Writing about his
brother may have enabled the poet to write about a part of himself
that might otherwise have been lost. The need to go back, to recover
in language what's lost, often impels poets to explore that landscape
of memory and early experiences. The dynamics of the families we
were given, before we could choose our own lives, seem to draw
many writers toward this material. Later, when family relationships
change—and when we begin families of our own of various kinds—
those closest to us still need to be written about, to be memorialized
and argued with and resented and loved.

IDEAS FOR WRITING

1. Divide a piece of paper with a long fold and head the two sides
   with the words "good" and "bad." On the "good" side, brainstorm
   a list of traits you have inherited for which you are glad or feel
   grateful. On the other side, list negative traits. Make the list as
   long as you like, but try for at least five on each side. Use this list
   to write a poem; address one or more members of your family.
   Steal Forché's lines to help you structure the poem: "I blame you
   for . . . But I'm glad . . . " Include a specific place name and give
   a sense of shared history.

2. Write about a gift your family, or someone in it, gave you. It might be an actual gift—a baseball glove, a book, a necklace—or a more intangible one. Talk about how that gift was or could be transferred to another, passed on.

3. Take out an old family photo and address the people in it or have them speak. Write about what's not in the frame: What happened before or after this picture was taken? What does the writer know now that the people in the photograph did not know then? Or try comparing two photographs—one past, one present. Consider what happened in the time between the two.

4. Compare an actual family photograph to one that was never taken, but might have been. Describe both photographs—the real and the imagined one—in detail.

5. Is there a particular person in your family with whom you feel in conflict? If so, write a poem in that person's voice, describing the relationship between you. Experience the other person's reality and way of seeing things, and then try to render that in the poem.

6. Read "My Mother Would Be A Falconress" by Robert Duncan, in his book *Bending the Bow* (it's also reprinted in several anthologies). Duncan uses and extends the metaphor throughout the poem to characterize a relationship between a mother and son. Write your own poem in which you develop a metaphor for your relationship with a parent or relative.

7. Describe an object that you associate with a particular family member. It might be a baby blanket, a pipe, a bathrobe, a hearing aid, a pair of eyeglasses, a black dress, anything that calls up that person for you. Talk about that object and, through your description of this person's use of it, create a portrait of his or her character.

8. Use a family anecdote, or a family ritual, as a leaping-off point for saying something about how your family or the world works. Read Louise Glück's "Spite and Malice" in *Ararat*, which uses a card game to talk about the dynamics of the family.

9. Is there a particular image, a particular moment, that seems to
   capture the essential spirit or character of someone in your family? Jot down an image, or a moment, for each person in your
   family. Pick the one that has the most energy for you, and begin
   a poem with that image.

Death and Grief

The mystery of death—whether one imagines it as a great nothing-ness, a transformation to another state, or a prelude to the next incar-nation—has inspired poets to some of their most profound meditations. Each of us has our own relationship to death, a rela-tionship that starts in childhood with our first awareness of it. And throughout our lives, we experience the grief and loss that another death brings. Writing can be a way of working through those emo-tions, an act of catharsis on the page. Poets are often people who *must* write in order to process their experiences and feelings; writing is, in a very real sense, a mode of perceiving the world, of taking it into our-selves as well as trying to externalize what's inside. Nothing can erase grief or speed up the process of healing, but writing can keep you aware as you go through it, and offer some solace. If you're dealing with a loss, we suggest that you keep a "grief journal"; write in it as often as possible, and use it as a vehicle for exploration.

Such writing, of course, may not result in terrific poetry; in fact, there's a good chance it won't. But it's probable that you'll find the seeds of poems when you're ready to go back to that raw place and try to shape something from it. Whether or not you return to the actual writing, you will have unearthed ideas, insights, questions, memories. These can be the starting points for poems that express your loss, or explore philosophical concerns, or vividly recreate those who have died.

Ours isn't a culture that accepts death or encourages much think-

ing about it. It's important that we as poets work to avoid such denial.
On whatever level you are presently concerned with death (and we
assume you are; after all, death is concerned with you), you should
feel free to write about it. Whether you are obsessed with the subject
of mortality, or consider it only occasionally, it can be a source of
moving and illuminating poetry.

This poem by Marie Howe asks us to consider what death might
feel like when it comes. Her strategy of addressing the reader makes
the sensations she imagines more vivid and personal:

DEATH, THE LAST VISIT

Hearing a low growl in your throat, you'll know that it's started.
It has nothing to ask you. It has only something to say, and
it will speak in your own tongue.

Locking its arm around you, it will hold you as long as you ever wanted.
Only this time it will be long enough. It will not let go.
Burying your face in its dark shoulder, you'll smell mud and hair and
    water.

You'll taste your mother's sour nipple, your favorite salty cock
and swallow a word you thought you'd spit out once and be done with.
Through half-closed eyes you'll see that its shadow looks like yours,

a perfect fit. You could weep with gratefulness. It will take you
as you like it best, hard and fast as a slap across your face,
or so sweet and slow you'll scream give it to me give it to me until it does.

Nothing will ever reach this deep. Nothing will ever clench this hard.
At last (the little girls are clapping, shouting) someone has pulled
the drawstring of your gym bag closed enough and tight. At last

someone has knotted the lace of your shoe so it won't ever come undone.
Even as you turn into it, even as you begin to feel yourself stop,
you'll whistle with amazement between your residual teeth oh jesus

oh sweetheart, oh holy mother, nothing nothing nothing ever felt this
    good.

Howe imagines death as a dynamic, powerful lover, the moment of dying as orgasm. Her descriptions are graphic and sexual. Death is an experience of unparalleled satisfaction, the tying up of all the messy loose ends of life. At the end of the poem, everything dissolves into bliss as the "you" cries out, addressing death in some of its various guises: "oh jesus / oh sweetheart, oh holy mother, nothing nothing nothing ever felt this good." As readers, we're startled and pleased by the intensity of Howe's poem, by its recognition of the ways that sex and death touch the same core. The writer doesn't try to sanitize death or gloss over it. The poem seduces us, so that we enter fully into the experience the poet has created for us. If we can't live forever, Howe's poem at least offers the possibility of death as a high point; personally, we hope she's right.

An *elegy*—from the Greek, *elegeia,* meaning lament—is a poem for the dead. It might be about someone who has died, or it might directly address that person. As its name suggests, the tone is likely to be sad or melancholy. Traditionally, elegies consider the meaning of death and seek some sort of consolation. One of our students once described the AIDS quilt as "a long poem"; with its colorful patchwork of names, of clothing and photographs and other mementos stitched together into a massive reminder of the disease's toll, the quilt is a powerful elegy.

Tess Gallagher's *Moon Crossing Bridge* was written after her husband, writer Raymond Carver, died of cancer. Here is one of the poems from that book:

WAKE

Three nights you lay in our house.
Three nights in the chill of the body.
Did I want to prove how surely
I'd been left behind? In the room's great dark
I climbed up beside you onto our high bed, bed
we'd loved in and slept in, married
and unmarried.

There was a halo of cold around you
as if the body's messages carry farther

> in death, my own warmth taking on the silver-white
> of a voice sent unbroken across snow just to hear
> itself in its clarity of calling. We were dead
> a little while together then, serene
> and afloat on the strange broad canopy
> of the abandoned world.

The moment Gallagher describes is a poignant one: climbing into bed with her dead husband. She describes the bed as the one "we'd loved in and slept in, married / and unmarried"; now the two are "unmarried" again, separated by death. She imagines "the body's messages" going on after death, herself calling across the coldness. The title could suggest not only the ritual of watching over a body before burial, but also what the poet would call to her love across that chill distance: "Wake!" For a short time she experiences the two of them as being the same, both "dead," both at peace.

Here's another poem that directly addresses a loved one who died. Poems of address often seek to convey a sense of intimacy; as a writer, you need to remember that a reader needs to know enough about the situation to feel that intimacy, and so feel the loss. Notice how Laurie Duesing helps the reader see the circumstances of this person's death, and how she uses the image of the stop watch—an ironic counterpoint to the tragic circumstances described.

PRECISION

for Brad Horrell, who died at Sears Point Raceway
on August 14, 1983

The day you flew in perfect arc
from your motorcycle was the same day
I broke the perfect formation of your women
at the railing, leaving behind
your grandmother and mother, to run
and jump the fence. The stop watch hanging
from my neck, suspended between gravity
and momentum, swung its perfect pendulum.

All our motion was brought to conclusion
by your broken body at rest
on the ground. Your breath never rose
to the oxygen placed on your face
and your heart never rallied
to the arms pressing your chest.
You wore the perfect clothes:
the ashy grey of death.

At the hospital they said your failure to survive
was complete. Though I never saw
the neck you perfectly broke or your body
cleanly draped by a sheet, I did see
your dead face bruising up at me
and for lack of something moving to touch,
I clutched the stop watch
which had not died.
If any nurse or doctor had asked,
I could have told, exactly,
to the hundredths of seconds, how long
it had been since I'd seen you alive.

Many poets have found that writing about someone's death rarely is finished in a single poem. Sharon Olds's *The Father* describes the last days of a father and the immediate aftermath of his death. Brenda Hillman's *The Death Tractates* is about the loss of a friend and mentor; Mark Doty's *My Alexandria* is imbued with the presence of AIDS, as are Thom Gunn's *The Man With Night Sweats* and Kenny Fries's *The Healing Notebooks*. In Alice Jones's *The Knot*, several poems deal with a former lover's death.

If you are writing about your own grief, don't try to get it all into one poem, to make some single pronouncement. Though death is a large subject, the way it enters our lives is often small: an object left behind, the memory of an offhand gesture made one long-ago afternoon, the smell of a T-shirt, the silly joke or absurd irony someone would have appreciated. In your writing, try to capture those intimate details that are the emblems of your particular loss.

IDEAS FOR WRITING

1. Write about the first experience with death that you can remember, whether it involved a person or an animal. Then write about your most recent experience with death. Combine the two in a poem.

2. Write a poem in which you speak after your own death. Imagine what death looks and feels like, what your emotions are. What advice can you give to the living?

3. Write a letter to someone who is dead. In it, make a confession.

4. In "Death, the Last Visit," Howe used the metaphor of a lover. Invent your own metaphor for death, and write a poem about what dying might feel like.

5. Who are your dead? Have them meet in a poem, even if they never met in life, and describe how they interact.

6. Read the newspaper and, when you find an account of a stranger's death that moves you, write an elegy for that person. Find a way that your life and that person's death are related, and talk about it in the poem.

7. Write a first-person poem in the voice of a public figure who is dead.

8. What can the dead do: go through walls, see the future, move objects? What are their powers and limitations? What are their desires, fears, pleasures? Describe them in a poem. (See Susan Mitchell's "The Dead" in Chapter 1.)

9. If you own some object that used to belong to someone who is no longer alive, describe it in detail, along with your memories or imaginings about how that person used it. You might also talk about how it is used in the present.

10. Write a poem about a ritual that accompanies a death. It might be about a traditional funeral, a wake, or some more private or individual observance. If you find an occasion for joy or beauty in the midst of mourning, include it. (Do this last part only if it feels true to your experience.)

Writing the Erotic

You've probably noticed, as we have, the proliferation of theme-based anthologies, ranging in subject matter from growing up Catholic to the poetry of the Vietnam war. Without a doubt one of the most anthologized subjects in recent years is the erotic. It shows up again and again in books with titles like *Deep Down, Touching Fire,* and *Best American Erotica,* to name only a few. The erotic has often been considered taboo, and even with the current abundance of sexual writing, it's under frequent attack. And yet the depiction of the erotic has a long and impressive history. It can be found in its earliest form as cave paintings, beautifully stylized and graphic images of the sexual act etched into stone with berry juice and ash, and later, in the Bible's lyrical and sensual "Song of Songs." Wherever there is human life, we find evidence of the erotic imagination. Poetry is a reflection of our lives and our imaginations, so it would seem that some of our best and most important poetry would be on this subject.

However, it's a difficult task to write openly and well about sex. When we asked our students what sorts of issues they struggled with in exploring erotic subject matter, the thing they mentioned most often was the language itself. It's frustrating to try and talk about sex with the language that's available to us. When we want to describe something as simple as bodies we find we are limited. Medical terminology is cold and clinical. The language of the street is a slang that is offensive to some, and certain terms may only be understood by the subculture that uses them. Euphemisms are intelligible to most but appreciated by few, least of all poets, who demand precision. And we are tired, as we should be, of the romantic clichés of the Victorian era: "her thighs were silk pillows" and "the glory of his manhood filled the room." How then do we create a new language that is capable of expressing our most intimate thoughts, feelings, and actions, and how do we describe an act which is so primal as to be preverbal, a wordless speech built on gestures, the senses, the flesh — the mute language of the body? Why is it that with our highly developed language skills we can describe, in complex and minute detail, how to assemble a sophisticated bomb, yet we have difficulty putting into words exactly what it is like to be a sexual creature?

We've found a number of contemporary poets who are discovering new ways to speak about the erotic. One is the gifted poet Sharon Olds. We suggest you read all five of her books, for pleasure first, of course, but secondly to examine how she goes about her difficult task. Here's a poem from her third book, *The Gold Cell*.

FIRST SEX

(For J.)

I knew little, and what I knew
I did not believe—they had lied to me
so many times, so I just took it as it
came, his naked body on the sheet,
the tiny hairs curling on his legs like
fine, gold shells, his sex
harder and harder under my palm
and yet not hard as a rock his face cocked
back as if in terror, the sweat
jumping out of his pores like sudden
trails from the tiny snails when his knees
locked with little clicks and under my
hand he gathered and shook and the actual
flood like milk came out of his body, I
saw it glow on his belly, all they had
said and more, I rubbed it into my
hands like lotion, I signed on for the duration.

This poem works on many levels, and for many reasons: it employs
the use of repetition, opposition, the surprising similes of the gold
shells and tiny snails, and the devices of rhythm and rhyme. But let's
take a closer look at the language itself. Re-read that third line: ". . .
so I just took it as it / came . . . " The word "came" used in the context of the line doesn't refer to sexual climax, but the word is there, to
conjure up the idea. And later, "his face cocked / back . . . " is used
to describe the angle of the man's face. In both cases, words or
phrases we attach to a sexual act have been slightly displaced. Also
notice how those words are emphasized by being positioned at the
beginning or end of the line. When the actual "climax" of the poem
occurs in the line "he gathered and shook," we are pleased and surprised by the similes describing the man's semen as "like milk," "like
lotion." On first reading we feel as if we've been given a rather
graphic description of the sexual act. But have we? Body parts are
mentioned: "his legs," "his sex," "palm," "face," "knees," "hand," and
"belly," even each tiny hair and pore in the skin, and yet there is no
feeling of vulgarity about the poem. What we feel is the magic, the
wonder and surprise of first sex, the strangeness of its sounds and
sights, the sensuality of it. We also sense the joy of it in the humor of
the last line which is emphasized by the use of rhyme: lotion / duration. Olds has shown us a way into this material by making use of the
old language in a new context. If you read more of her poetry about
sex, you'll find this sort of displacement throughout.

This strategy has been used by other poets as well; the following
poem by Kate Daniels employs the language of *Eros* to depict its
aftermath:

BATHING

He always bathed afterwards,
slipping his fine and sticky
genitals over the cool rim
of the porcelain sink.
She lay in the other room
smoking and staring tiredly
out the window. The tiny sounds

of the suds came to her
worrisomely. The *suck-suck*
sound of his hand lathering
soap into his tight, dark curls.
Then the farewell groan of the drain.
The energetic flap of the towel.
When he was before her again,
his teeth covered by a smile,
the sweat and stench removed,
she studied him from the crushed
bed, admiring his cruel
beauty, her body still marked
and odorous. His, clean
and unstained, amnesiac
already.

Notice how words that might describe the sexual intimacy of two people are used here to intensify the awareness that the man's intimacy is not with the woman, but with his separateness. "Slipping," "the *suck-suck* / sound of his hand," "groan," are all related to the man's solitary actions; they lend an added poignancy to this bleak vision of the couple's relationship.

Another way into the erotic is through the window of imagery. Brenda Hillman writes of the memory of teenage sexuality in a poem called "The Spark." Here's an excerpt:

. . . .

Start the memory, bright one,
you who let your life be invented
though not being invented had been more available

and remember those
who lit the abyss. The boys in science fair.
You were probably hall monitor at that time weren't you,
and you admired them;
on their generator, the spark bounced back and forth
like baby lightning
and you saw them run their fingertips

through its danger,
two promising loops stuck up to provide
a home for the sexual light
which was always loose when it wasn't broken,
free joy that didn't go anywhere
but moved between the wires
like a piece of living, in advance —

then later: how much
were you supposed to share?
The boys sat in front of your house at dusk,
the boys who still had parents.
Sometimes they held Marlboros out the car
windows and even
if they didn't, sparks fell from their hands.
Showers of sparks
between nineteen sixty-eight and the

hands were sleek
with asking sleek with asking; —

they had those long intermural after
the library type fingers
they would later put in you, —ah.
When? well,
when they had talked you into having a body
they could ask into the depths of

and they rose to meet you
against an ignorance that made you perfect
and you rose to meet them like a waitress of fire —

because: didn't
the spark shine best in the bodies
under the mild shooting stars
on the back-and-forth blanket
from the fathers' cars —
they lay down with you, in you, and when
did you start missing them.
As Sacramento missed its yellow dust 1852.

When did you start missing those
who invented your body with their sparks—

they didn't mind being
plural. They put
their summer stars inside of you,

how nice to have. and then:
the pretty soon. Pretty
soon you were a body, space, warm
flesh warm (this)
(this) under
the summer meteors that fell
like lower case i's above
the cave of granite where the white owl slept

without because or why
what first evening of the world . . .

Hillman uses the image of sparks, as well as the manifestations of fire, lightning, stars, and meteors, to transport us through imagery to a world of sexuality and desire. Each image supports or extends the next: the boys running their fingers through the generator sparks, later putting those same fingers inside the girl, and then putting the "summer stars" of their semen inside the girl's body. The images are graphic, even more so than anything in the Olds poem, but because the sexual images are tied together with images of the natural world, they feel instinctive, right. Even the landscape becomes eroticized in the image of a meteor shower falling over a cave.

Metaphor can be another way of writing about the erotic, as it is in this four-line poem by Jane Hirshfield:

THE GROUNDFALL PEAR

It is the one he chooses,
yellow, plump, a little bruised
on one side from falling.
That place he takes first.

Notice how quickly and simply the pear in this poem has become eroticized. It is chosen, like a woman or man is "chosen"; there is no need even to pluck it from the tree. It is simply there—beautiful, available, fat, ripe, and ready to eat. The idea of "forbidden fruit" is conjured up, as is the idea of the fall from grace. And what is most desired is the spot that is evidence of the fall, the place of impact, that "little bruise." The erotic is transgressive, forbidden; eating rotting food, taking without asking, are taboos the poem subtly evokes. Hirshfield finds her eroticism by writing off or away from the subject—not to avoid it, but to take an unexpected path toward it. Maybe that's why metaphor can be so erotic: fulfilled desire, the thing itself, is not as erotic as our yearning toward it. There needs to be a little distance, a gap, an Other. Figurative language can call forth that yearning, but keep the object always just tantalizingly beyond our reach.

But what if we do want to approach the subject head-on? What if our desire is to be direct and graphic—can it be done? We haven't found an overwhelming number of poems that approach the erotic with truly graphic language, but there are some. Marilyn Hacker, for example, has some explicit sonnets about lesbian sex in Bloomingdales and other exotic locations. It seems to us that more prose writers than poets are exploring the edge, using the language and structures of pornography in new ways, creating texts that are deliberately transgressive and that expand the boundaries of what's permissible. However, David Trinidad, who writes poems about sexuality from a gay man's perspective, does so in very explicit terms. Here's an excerpt from a poem in several sections, "Eighteen to Twenty-One":

V

Tom used spit for lubricant and fucked me
on the floor of his Volkswagen van while
his ex-lover (also named Tom) drove and
watched (I was sure) in the rearview mirror. . . .

Such sexual frankness in poems is not, as we've said, particularly common. (Maybe we've been reading the wrong people, though, and missing something.) But in any case, it's certainly an option. Some people may be troubled by the use of graphic language, but exploring the source of our reticence about using certain words can be useful to us as writers. You may find that you're embarrassed to talk about particular intimacies—or you may feel liberated by the possibilities. Reading and writing erotic poems can be, well, exciting. Whether you're drawn to soft sensuality or raw transgression, the territory of the body, of sexuality in all its manifestations, is still open for exploration.

IDEAS FOR WRITING

1. Do a ten–minute, uncensored freewrite on incidents from your past (or someone else's) that relate to some erotic discovery you, or they, made earlier in life. Choose one from your list and use "First Sex" as a model for writing your own poem. Try for some displaced language.

2. Brainstorm a list of mundane activities not usually thought of as erotic—washing the dishes or the car, mowing the lawn, going to the dentist. Now, make a list of nouns associated with that activity. Then make a list of verbs and adjectives that you associate with sex. Stir everything together, and make the mundane activity sound positively orgasmic.

3. Do the above exercise, but this time eroticize a landscape, like Hillman. A field or rocky bluff will do, but also try something nontraditional—a scrapyard, an empty parking lot. Again, draw your nouns from the landscape, your verbs and adjectives from sexual words.

4. Make a list of what's erotic to you: parts of the body, traditional and nontraditional; foods, objects, clothing, words, smells, sounds. Pick seven to ten words from your various categories and make a poem out of them.

5. Begin a poem with the phrase "I want" or "Tonight I want . . . " and use things from the lists you made in the previous exercise. If you get stuck, keep repeating your "I want."

6. Collect images from magazines that turn you on (the journal *Yellow Silk* is usually filled with beautiful paintings and photographs), or buy a handful of erotic postcards. Choose an image that particularly appeals to you and really study it. Then write a poem, using any of the strategies described below:

    Begin with a precise description of the image, but then link what is there to something else—let it trigger a memory, an idea about love or the erotic, a fantasy.

    Address the people/objects pictured. Ask questions of the image. Allow the people or objects to speak; give them a voice.

    Describe what might have gone on just before or just after the scene depicted in the painting or photograph. (Remember those old jump cuts in movies where the man and woman are embracing or kissing, and the next scene shows them eating breakfast the next morning? Fill in what happens—or what you want to have happen.)

7. Using "Groundfall Pear" as a model, write a four or five line poem that is a metaphor for sex, desire, love.

8. Read "homage to my hips" by Lucille Clifton in the "Voice and Style" chapter and then write a sexy homage to a body part.

9. Write a pornographic poem—that is, one you think is pornographic. Define it for yourself; we won't begin to attempt to talk about the difference between "erotic" and "pornographic," except to say that the best definition we ever heard was this: "Erotica is what I like. Pornography is what *you* like."

10. Read all of David Trinidad's "Eighteen to Twenty-One" (printed in the anthology *High Risk*), and write your own sexual history, or a part of it.

11. Write a poem to a particular lover—or would-be lover—designed to make him or her wild with passion. Describe exactly what you're going to do, wear, say, and so on. Then send it to that person. We dare you.

The Shadow

According to the psychologist Carl Jung, each of us has a daily, more pleasant self with which we identify—our ego—and a hidden self which we tend to reject and deny—what is known as our shadow. While the division into ego and shadow comes from Jung, it's an idea that humankind has recognized for centuries and that we all immediately understand: that the self is both dark and light, that the world contains both good and evil.

Our personal shadow lies in the unconscious and is formed when we are young, when we learn to identify with what our culture tells us are acceptable behaviors, thoughts, emotions. Poet Robert Bly calls the shadow "the long bag we drag behind us," explaining that as we learn what others don't like or accept in us we start "bag-stuffing." By the time we reach adulthood, Bly says, there is only a "thin slice" of us left—the rest is in that long bag.

The problem is that while the shadow is necessary to the formation of who we are, we end up denying its existence, or at best fearing it. And that denial causes problems, because the dark side of ourselves contains not only what we consider negative traits but also our undeveloped talents and gifts. We all have powerful creative energies locked inside; to deny them is to deny the possibility of wholeness.

On a larger scale, entire societies have their shadow, which they are busy suppressing. When we refuse to acknowledge the shadow we not only lose the chance to integrate it, but risk being dominated by it. Coming to terms with both our personal shadow and the collective one is one of the important ways the artist can function in relation to his or her own art, and in relation to his or her culture. The artist can try to show the culture issues it doesn't want to look at, can explore those frightening areas of the psyche. The French novelist Colette said, "Look hard at what pleases you and harder at what doesn't." Poets can't afford to be "nice" if they're to explore the more troubling realms of human experience.

Does this mean that poems shouldn't be beautiful? Of course not. Light is important. Affirmation is important. Poetry isn't all about wars and unhappy childhoods and failed love affairs—and shouldn't be. But we've encountered a number of people who have difficulty with going deeper, who splash in the shallows and never dive down into the scary, murky depths—and their poetry reflects that. They have trouble accessing that deeper self, so that when they write they are constantly, consciously *thinking*: "Where am I going next? Is that the right grammar? Does this make sense? Is this too weird? Who's going to read this after I've written it?" Such thoughts can stop the creative impulse dead in its tracks. And the writing that results is likely to be tepid, perhaps pretty, but ultimately unsuccessful in conveying something meaningful about human experience.

How can you gain access to the shadow, and mine it for poetry? It's important to get past the voices that tell you what you "should" write, the voices that say you want people to like you, to think you are a good person—the "writing as seduction" school. It means going into territory that may be labeled "forbidden," or that may be personally difficult. It's important not to censor yourself. Give yourself permission to explore wherever the writing takes you. Of course, this kind of writing—going towards what is hardest to speak of, whether that's the suffering in the world or your own personal obsessions—takes a certain amount of courage. Your normal, denying self doesn't want to deal with those things. But sometimes, writing may be the only place you can express them. There's a great feeling of relief and catharsis when you manage to get something that's been buried or hidden out onto the page. And such a process, whether or not it eventually results in a poem, helps to integrate that part of the self.

Many poets have struggled with that chaotic, difficult part of their psyche, and some of their writing has been about their personal demons. John Berryman, Randall Jarrell, Anne Sexton—these were some of an earlier generation of American writers who coped variously with depression, alcohol or drug dependency, deep-rooted self-destructive urges. We aren't suggesting that mental instability or unhappiness makes one a better poet, or a poet at all; and contrary to the romantic notion of the artist suffering for his or her work, we think these writers achieved brilliance in spite of their suffering, not because of it. Still, Jung also said that there were no heights without the corresponding depths; and these poets reached deeply into themselves.

Jane Kenyon writes about depression in her poem "Having It Out With Melancholy." Here is the first of the nine sections:

I. FROM THE NURSERY

When I was born, you waited
behind a pile of linen in the nursery,
and when we were alone, you lay down
on top of me, pressing
the bile of desolation into every pore.

And from that day on
everything under the sun and moon
made me sad—even the yellow
wooden beads that slid and spun
along a spindle on my crib.

You taught me to exist without gratitude.
You ruined my manners toward God:
"We're here simply to wait for death;
the pleasures of earth are overrated."

I only appeared to belong to my mother,
to live among blocks and cotton undershirts
with snaps; among red tin lunch boxes
and report cards in ugly brown slipcases.

> I was already yours—the anti-urge,
> the mutilator of souls.

Kenyon addresses "the anti-urge," the weight of depression which, the narrator claims, has pressed down on her since childhood. In another section she calls it "a crow who smells hot blood," which arrives "to pull me out / of the glowing stream" just when she has managed to feel, briefly, a sense of connection with all of humanity. Later, she describes how it feels to live in such a state of psychic misery:

> A piece of burned meat
> wears my clothes, speaks
> in my voice, dispatches obligations
> haltingly, or not at all.
> It is tired of trying
> to be stouthearted, tired
> beyond measure.

> (*from* part 7., PARDON)

By the end of the poem, the narrator has managed to come to a hard-won but fragile truce with that other that lives inside of herself; and her readers have taken the journey with her.

We think that, for poets, integrating the shadow side also means training yourself to *see*. We once gave an assignment in which we were focusing on the making of images—creating vivid, evocative, sensual descriptions of things in the world. It was suggested that everyone describe a homeless man or woman and render him or her in such graphic detail that each of us could conjure up this person before us in the classroom. One woman had difficulty with the assignment because, she said, "I never really looked at a homeless person closely." Poets need to train themselves to look closely at the world, to observe it carefully and continuously.

In this next poem Corrine Hales makes us look closely at a commonplace domestic scene which immediately makes us uneasy, even before the terrible act at the heart of the poem is revealed.

SUNDAY MORNING

Crowded around the glowing open mouth
Of the electric oven, the children
Pull on clothes and eat brown-sugared oatmeal.

The broiler strains, buzzing to keep up
500 degrees, and the mother
Is already scrubbing at a dark streak

On the kitchen wall. Last night she'd been
Ironing shirts and trying her best to explain
Something important to the children

When the old mother cat's surviving
Two kittens' insistent squealing and scrambling
Out of their cardboard box began

To get to her. The baby screamed every time
The oldest girl set him on the cold floor
While she carried a kitten back to its place

Near the stove, and the mother cat kept reaching
For the butter dish on the table. Twice, the woman
Stopped talking and set her iron down to swat

A quick kitten away from the dangling cord,
And she saw that one of the boys had begun to feed
Margarine to his favorite by the fingerful.

When it finally jumped from his lap and squatted
To piss on a pale man's shirt dropped below
Her ironing board, the woman calmly stopped, unplugged

Her iron, picked up the gray kitten with one hand
And threw it, as if it were a housefly, hard
And straight at the yellow flowered wall

Across the room. It hit, cracked, and seemed to slide
Into a heap on the floor, leaving an odd silence
In the house. They all stood still

Staring at the thing, until one child,
The middle boy, walked slowly out of the room

And down the hall without looking

At his mother or what she'd done. The others followed
And by morning everything was back to normal
Except for the mother standing there scrubbing.

This is a poem we grow uncomfortable reading; like the boy who leaves the room, we don't want to look. But Hales has engaged us already; by the time we get to the mother's violent act, it's too late. Worse, we even feel a bit complicit with her. Anyone who's been around little children knows how they can strain one's patience to the breaking point; we can see this frazzled woman trying to deal with kids and animals and just losing it. This is the dangerous underside of the family, and it's not a pleasant experience to read about it.

We believe that to be a poet means that as a person, you must be willing to feel the emotions that come from facing the world, and your particular truths about it, unflinchingly. You may be able to craft gorgeously cadenced lines, full of fresh, surprising metaphor, sonorous combinations of words, and multilayered allusions—but all this, without *seeing*, will only produce what we might call pseudo-poems. They may be very good, by current standards—many of them find their way into respected literary journals. But true poems, and poets, are difficult to come by. They have to have what the Spanish call *duende*—what poet Federico Garcia Lorca described as "the mystery, the roots that probe through the mire that we all know of, and do not understand, but which furnishes us with whatever is sustaining in art." Lorca defines *duende* by quoting the German writer Goethe: "A mysterious power that all may feel and no philosophy can explain." What matters in your work, ultimately, is not how much it pleases an editor, but whether it has integrity—integrity of vision as much as language.

IDEAS FOR WRITING

1. As a warmup, write something that you would never show to anyone, that you are afraid even to put down on the page. Get it out, as much of it as possible, in as much shameful or horrifying detail as you can manage. Afterwards, feel free to tear it up or burn it; the exercise is successful if it has enabled you to get in touch with that place in yourself.

2. What repels you—the smell of garbage? Sloppiness? People who never shut up? Make a list of things you dislike intensely. Choose one or more and try to transform them into something appealing or beautiful.

3. What positive qualities do you consider are part of your personality? Are you a good listener? Generous to your friends? Concerned about the suffering in the world? Take a trait that you are proud of and find the opposite trait within yourself. Write a poem describing and exploring all the ways you are not a good listener, are selfish, and so on. (We got the idea for this from a line by Sharon Olds: "And what if I am not good, what if I am a taker?")

4. Imagine that your shadow has a name, a face, certain habits, likes and dislikes. Describe your shadow. Then describe what your shadow's reactions are to a particular action you perform—such as tucking in a child, making love, going for a walk, writing a poem.

5. What would you consider a taboo subject for a poem? (You may think of several things.) Now break your own taboo—transgress. If you feel very uncomfortable doing this, you're on the right track.

6. Write a "confession" poem detailing an emotional crime and how you committed it.

7. Write a poem in the voice of a murderer. Make the reader sympathetic to the murderer.

8. Write a poem about an incident which caused you to feel a sense of shame.

9. Take a negative aspect of the self—fear or depression or paralysis or cruelty—and find a concrete image for what it feels like. Remember Kenyon's "black crow." Maybe it is like the weight she describes pressing down; or like walking into an abandoned house; or sinking into a deep chair; or slogging through mud. Once you settle on your topic and the image for it, develop that image in a poem titled "Fear," "Depression," etc.

10. The traditional imagery for good and evil is light and dark, white and black. Brainstorm a list of images called up by the two opposites, light/white and black/dark. Then write a poem that inverts and reverses those traditional associations. That is, what is beautiful, fertile, inspiring in the dark, in night, in deep caves? What's awful or terrifying in daylight?

Witnessing

What kind of times are they, when
A talk about trees is almost a crime
Because it implies silence about so many horrors?
—Bertolt Brecht,
"To Those Born Later"

The German poet and playwright wrote those lines in the thirties, but what he called the "dark times" are far from over. It seems we have always lived in dark times; from the beginning of human history, war and turmoil—over possessions, land, religion, grievances great and trivial—have accompanied our so-called progress as a species. Today we are no more enlightened; this century has seen destruction on a greater scale than at any other time in history.

Writing a poem in such times may feel a little like fiddling while Rome burns. Yet we're poets. Writing is what we do in the world—or part of it anyway—and as ephemeral as it might sometimes seem, the making of poems is a necessary act, one that allies itself with hope rather than despair.

Language is a power that is used in many ways. Advertising exploits language to convince us we are buying not only a product but a bit of class, or sexiness, or sophistication. Politicians hire speechwriters to play on our sense of patriotism, our fears, our compassion for others. Read George Orwell's famous essay "Politics and the English Language," or his classic novel, *1984*. Political doublespeak is everywhere. In a war, a phrase like "collateral damage" may be used to refer to civilian casualties. But even the words "civilian casualties" create a screen beyond which it's hard to see real human suffering. Poems, on the other hand, use language to tell the truth, to accurately portray someone's experience or vision; that's the source of their power, and of their effects on the world.

In a sense, all poems are poems of witness. They record what it's like to be alive, set down what is passing and irrecoverable. They say *this happened*, or *this is what it felt like*, or *this is who I am, who she was, what they stood for*. And also, of course, *this is what never happened, according to a person who will never exist*; those poems bear witness to the imagination, to the endless human capacity for creative invention. But we want to talk about witness in a more particular way. A poem of witness is the opposite of Brecht's "talk about trees"; it wants to look at the realities and name them, to retrieve them from the silence. It tends to look, not inward at the self, but outward to the connections between self and world, toward the social and historical.

Carolyn Forché, in the introduction to her excellent and moving anthology *Against Forgetting: Twentieth Century Poetry of Witness*, talks about the limits of categories such as "personal" and "political" when applied to poetry. She talks about "the social" as the "space between the state and the supposedly safe havens of the personal," and later says, "The poetry of witness reclaims the social from the political and in so doing defends the individual against illegitimate forms of coercion." Perhaps this could be extended to include not only defense of the individual, but defense of the earth, the environment, and the other inhabitants of the planet, the animals.

The poets in *Against Forgetting* are all personal witnesses, people who coped with extreme conditions such as war, imprisonment, torture. Yet one needn't be personally subjected to such conditions to feel strongly about suffering and to write about it. As poets, we need to write from our experience, but that experience may be mental, emotional, and imaginative as well as physical. Our link to the suffering of others is that we care about it, and what we care about we tend to put into our writing. There's no reason to inject "political"

content into your work because you feel you should be writing about
something "important." Conversely, there are writers who get stuck
in the personal, scarcely looking up from their carefully tended garden of self-absorption. It seems to us that any aware human being is
going to look beyond that garden at some point. But a poem about a
worker poisoned by asbestos isn't inherently better than one about a
lover. Subject matter is not the issue; depth of imagination, and its
articulation in language, is.

In his poem "Dedication," Nobel Laureate Czeslaw Milosz wrote,
"What is poetry which does not save / Nations or people? / A con-
nivance with official lies, / A song of drunkards whose throats will be
cut in a moment . . . " In an interview in *Poets & Writers* magazine,
Milosz discussed his thoughts on those words, and suggested that
"what those lines mean is that poetry below a certain awareness is not
good poetry and cannot save people, that we move, that mankind
moves in time together and then there is a certain awareness of a particular moment below which we shouldn't go, because then that
poetry is no good . . . So it's a question of awareness that shapes our
poetry, even if poetry doesn't deal with direct political topics or historical topics." Besides this, there are the words of Adrienne Rich in
her poem "North American Time": "Poetry never stood a chance / of
standing outside history."

Suppose, though, that you do want to deal with those political or
historical topics, somewhere, somehow, in your poetry. Whether
you've endured something personally, or know people who have, or
want to address or to speak for strangers, you will need to fully inhabit
the material so that you don't slip into easy rhetoric or soapbox
preaching. Admittedly the largeness of such issues, their size and
complexity, can leave you feeling somewhat lost in terms of how to
approach them. The important thing here is to look at your personal
truths—not to try and present a comprehensive portrait of the injus-
tice in the world. Describe your own experience, or imagine that of
others, at the level of the human. Let readers in, instead of shutting
them out with the thunder of your convictions and commitment. In
spite of vast cultural differences, there is, at bottom, some common
ground for all of us. Finding that commonality in your poems will

bring home the larger issues, render them in terms of their conse-
quences: no "collateral damage" without an understanding of its
effects on someone, a stranger whom under other circumstances you
might have loved, and mourned—or who might, in the next slight
shift between the forces of dark and light, become yourself.

This poem by Linda Hogan begins with a description of a place the
narrator has just moved into, but quickly opens out from the local.
The specific place dissolves, as do the boundaries between self and
other, the living and the dead. Like Walt Whitman, who in "Song of
Myself" claimed "I am large, I contain multitudes," the poet seems to
contain not only her Native American ancestors but the lives of others around her, neighbors and strangers. There's a constant interplay
between inner and outer, the mundane and the magical. There is
anger in the poem, and compassion, and historical memory, all presented with a simple and undramatic clarity.

THE NEW APARTMENT: MINNEAPOLIS

The floorboards creak.
The moon is on the wrong side of the building,

and burns remain
on the floor.

The house wants to fall down
the universe when earth turns.

It still holds the coughs of old men
and their canes tapping on the floor.

I think of Indian people here before me
and how last spring white merchants hung an elder

on a meathook and beat him
and he was one of The People.

I remember this war
and all the wars

and relocation like putting the moon in prison
with no food and that moon already a crescent,

but be warned, the moon grows full again
and the roofs of this town are all red

and we are looking through the walls of houses
at people suspended in air.

Some are baking, with flour on their hands,
or sleeping on floor three, or getting drunk.

I see the businessmen who hit their wives
and the men who are tender fathers.

There are women crying or making jokes.
Children are laughing under beds.

Girls in navy blue robes talk on the phone all night
and some Pawnee is singing 49s, drumming the table.

Inside the walls
world changes are planned, bosses overthrown.

If we had no coffee,
cigarettes, or liquor,

says the woman in room twelve,
they'd have a revolution on their hands.

Beyond walls are lakes and plains,
canyons and the universe;

the stars are the key
turning in the lock of night.

Turn the deadbolt and I am home.
I have walked dark earth,

opened a door to nights where there are no apartments,
just drumming and singing;

The Duck Song, The Snake Song,
The Drunk Song.

No one here remembers the city
or has ever lost the will to go on.

Hello aunt, hello brothers, hello trees
and deer walking quietly on the soft red earth.

The speaker in this poem feels a strong bond with those who came before; at the end of the poem she becomes one with them, with the trees and animals, expressing a more wholistic vision of life behind the fragmented one presented by the alienating urban landscape. Witnessing involves the past as well as the present; it's crucial that we explore who we came from, where we came from, what happened. This is true for all peoples, for without the past, without memory, there is no culture, and no tradition to be passed on. Poetry has always functioned as a way to remember. Maybe that's one reason why it's been so undervalued in a culture which prefers amnesia, today's celebrity scandal or political corruption blotting out yesterday's, the new bulldozing the old. A character in one of Czech novelist Milan Kundera's books says that the struggle against power "is the struggle of memory against forgetting."

There's a vast difference, of course, between memory and nostalgia—a sentimental longing for what never was. Memory is as likely to be painful as pleasant, and writers who explore its territory, whether on a personal or wider cultural level, must be willing to present its sometimes difficult truths. This poem by Bruce Weigl, which details an individual's memories of the Vietnam war, confronts the persistence of painful memories and the difficulty of finding solace, even while the narrator yearns for relief.

SONG OF NAPALM

for my wife

> After the storm, after the rain stopped pounding,
> We stood in the doorway watching horses
> Walk off lazily across the pasture's hill.
> We stared through the black screen,
> Our vision altered by the distance
> So I thought I saw a mist
> Kicked up around their hooves when they faded
> Like cut-out horses
> Away from us.
> The grass was never more blue in that light, more
> Scarlet; beyond the pasture
> Trees scraped their voices into the wind, branches

Criss-crossed the sky like barbed wire
But you said they were only branches.

Okay. The storm stopped pounding.
I am trying to say this straight: for once
I was sane enough to pause and breathe
Outside my wild plans and after the hard rain
I turned my back on the old curses. I believed
They swung finally away from me . . .

But still the branches are wire
And thunder is the pounding mortar,
Still I close my eyes and see the girl
Running from her village, napalm
Stuck to her dress like jelly,
Her hands reaching for the no one
Who waits in waves of heat before her.

So I can keep on living,
So I can stay here beside you,
I try to imagine she runs down the road and wings
Beat inside her until she rises
Above the stinking jungle and her pain
Eases, and your pain, and mine.

But the lie swings back again.
The lie works only as long as it takes to speak
And the girl runs only as far
As the napalm allows
Until her burning tendons and crackling
Muscles draw her up
Into that final position
Burning bodies so perfectly assume. Nothing
Can change that; she is burned behind my eyes
And not your good love and not the rain-swept air
And not the jungle green
Pasture unfolding before us can deny it.

Weigl's poem holds redemption and horror eternally balanced;
there is the beauty of the horses in that pasture, the "good love" of the

wife, while at the same time the image of the napalmed girl is "burned" into memory. Though the poem is of one man's experience, it speaks to us of all those who have survived war and continually struggle to come to terms with such images. Notice how Weigl interweaves past and present: the horses are seen through a "black screen"—a barrier, but a permeable one. The "pounding" of the storm becomes pounding mortar, the branches are barbed wire, and the pasture is "jungle green." The poem is about language, too, and reminds us that language can lie; with the power of words, the poet can make the girl, for an instant, grow angelic wings and escape. Language, though, finally fails him; it can't save either the girl or himself.

We said earlier that you don't have to have experienced extremity to write poems of witness. Perhaps, like Hogan, your link is through ancestry, the poverty or oppression of members of your family, or race, or religion. Many Jewish writers have felt moved to explore the Holocaust. But so have writers whose religion and history would seem far removed from the killing of millions of Jews. Such writers identified with that suffering, not as Jews, but as human beings. Hearing how children were separated from their parents at the camps, a poet who is a parent might easily imagine the anguish of having his or her child taken away. You might have read William Styron's novel *Sophie's Choice* or seen the film; such a scene is at the heart of it (interestingly, the main character is not Jewish, but Catholic). Norman Dubie wrote a stunning poem in the voice of a black woman slave who escapes to the north ("The Negress: Her Monologue of Dark and Light"), and it convincingly and compellingly portrays her physical and emotional journey. Sharon Olds has written of starvation, civil rights, suicide, abandoned babies— without herself living through drought, risking lynching, or otherwise physically participating in those events. The imagination is free to follow whatever subject matter it finds compelling. To say otherwise— that, say, a man can't speak as a woman, or an African-American as a Polish Jew, or a lesbian mother as Don Juan—is to impoverish us all. You may want to bear witness to your own experience, but try not to define that experience too narrowly.

IDEAS FOR WRITING

1. What issues in the world concern you? Write a rant; be as rhetorical as you like, get up on your soapbox and scream. Once that's out of your system, you're ready to begin a poem. Explore a large issue—racism, sexism, violence, war, vanishing wildlife. Find out how and where that issue enters your life, intersects with it. Make it personal: the story in the newspaper on your kitchen table, next to the plate of eggs; the homeless person sitting next to the Coke machine outside the grocery store; a walk in the woods; a remembered incident from childhood.

2. The poet James Merrill wrote, "we understand history through the family around the table." In what ways does your own family story overlap with the story of others—an ethnic group, a historical event, a social issue? Write a poem about someone in your family and how his or her story is related to history.

3. Take a newspaper account of an incident—a riot, an assassination, a bombing—and imagine that you are one of the participants. Rewrite the account as a first-person poem, using some of the details from the account.

4. Objects have histories, too. Take an object and research its social history; where did it come from? How was it used, developed, made? What groups of people used it, misused it? Write a poem talking about what you've found. A wonderful poem you should look at is Robert Pinsky's "Shirt" in his book *The Want Bone*.

5. Imagine someone who lives in another part of the world under very different economic and political circumstances. Have that person talk about your life in America from his or her perspective. You can also do this exercise by imagining someone else in America, but of a different class, race, and so forth.

6. Everyone of a certain age remembers where they were when John F. Kennedy was assassinated. Think about where you were when some major event occurred; write a poem that draws a parallel between something in your life and the event.

7. What communities of people do you identify with and feel you belong to? Write a poem from the voice of this collective "we," talking about your troubles, your failings, celebrating your strengths.

8. In what ways do you feel oppressed? Privileged? Choose an object you own that seems to embody that oppression and/or privilege, and write a poem about it. It could be anything: a car, a lipstick, a tie, a photograph.

9. Write a poem that is a conversation between you and a politically powerful figure from any moment in history. The person can be living or dead; you must have a question you want to ask this person, and ask it in the poem. Let the person answer the question, too; make it a true conversation.

10. Remember John Lennon's "Imagine"? What would your ideal world look like? Write a poem that begins, "Imagine . . . " and let yourself dream. Remember, though, that you'll need to stay specific — "Imagine no war" sounds great in a song, but won't cut it as poetry. How would "no war" look in concrete terms? Offer an alternative vision. You don't need to cover everything that's wrong in the world; choose one thing, to start.

Poetry of Place

When we imagine the birch trees and wooded hills of New England, we remember the poems of Robert Frost and Donald Hall. We can't think of the poetry of Garrett Hongo or Cathy Song without envisioning the hibiscus flowers and volcanoes of Hawaii. The name Philip Levine calls up Detroit, its car factories, its black clouds and slick rivers.

When we hear the word "landscape," we tend to think of poems about nature: hills, valleys, forests, and animal life, and those things are certainly part of it. Poets like Mary Oliver and John Haines have given us their visions of the natural world. But a landscape includes any vision of place: the heated rhythms of the city, the long silences of the desert, the pastel houserows and clipped lawns of the suburbs, the sights, sounds, and smells of our neighborhoods that help to shape our imagination and build the foundation on which to compare all landscapes that follow. Often, where we grew up is not where we are now. The landscape of our childhood may be literally lost—familiar streets and family businesses bulldozed for condos or shopping malls. Or it may be far away—in another state, another country—but that place remains in our memory. Where we come from, where we live now, the particular places that are ours, help to define us, and influence and inform our poetry.

Robert Winner was born in the Bronx in 1930. A spinal cord injury at the age of sixteen kept him in a wheelchair until his death in 1986.

The Sanity of Earth and Grass, his complete poems, sounds from its title like a book of nature poetry. It's in fact a book which often evokes the city where he lived: the landscape of the Bronx. Here's how one poem begins:

HOME

My heart and my bones wince.
It's so damn sad-looking
and ugly, the Bronx—
driving past those small hills
blighted for miles with bleak
six-story desert-like apartment
buildings—the landscape I come from.
It's so damn ugly in its torment
of knifings and fires, I forget
I was happy there sometimes
in its damp and dingy streets, living my life
with the five continents of the world
in my mind's eye.

Maybe it was beautiful before us:
the coast with no landfill
a bluffed peninsula of swamps and forests,
a wilderness that became another wilderness
—beds and linoleum, school books,
musty hallways, laughter, despondency—
unremembering earth, a riverbed
millions flowed on, clinging briefly
to some masonry, then gone . . .

. . . .

Winner's childhood landscape is unsentimentalized; there's none of the easy nostalgia one might expect from the title "Home." Instead, it's "a wilderness that became another wilderness." Every landscape is a frontier, a place of energy and discovery for the people who inhabit it. It can also be a gateway into our internal and emotional lives. Look at this poem by Charlie Smith:

THE PALMS

When the sun went down in L.A. that day I was driving
a rental car east on Sunset Boulevard,
worn down by the endless internal battering,
and looked back to see the vivid capacious burned oceanic light,
the dust in the air that made the light palpable and beautiful
hanging over the pastel city, and saw the crunched little stores
with their brocades of steel locking them up
and the narrow streets springing downhill like madmen
running away; and there was a ridge that blocked the sun,
a scruffy torn wall of yellow earth with a few small houses on top,
widely spaced, disconnected-looking, though down from them
there was a neighborhood of bunched-up shacks
and a street that wound through patches of willow and bouganvillea;
and on the ridge that was sharply defined by the
rotted unmanageable light, there were a few palm trees,
untouched at that moment by breeze so that their tops
hung limply; and they seemed, black against the huge sky
of Los Angeles, like small dark thoughts tethered
at the end of reason's thick ropes, hanging there in gratuitous solitude,
like the thoughts of a man behind a cluttered restaurant counter,
who speaks no English, wearing a hat made of butcher paper,
who slaps and slaps his small daughter, until they both are stunned,
stupid and helpless, overwhelmed by their lives.

   The landscape of Los Angeles has given Smith a starting point for
a poem about the "endless internal battering" that is wearing down
the narrator. The images Smith describes correspond to the narrator's
emotional turmoil, his exhaustion; we could say either that he pro-
jects his agitation onto the landscape, or that he finds his inner state
reflected in the actual world. The palm trees are "untouched,"
"limp," "black against the huge sky." In another state of mind the
same trees might look stalwart, hopeful, or merely melancholy,
instead of completely insignificant and isolated. This is one way to
use landscape, and it captures a truth about how the world works on
us and how we, in turn, create it.
   Richard Hugo used the word "trigger" to define the thing that hap-

pens when we become inspired to write a poem. Hugo was often inspired by a town, especially one he had never seen before and was only passing through. The town would spark his imagination: Who lives here? What do they do all day? Why did they leave that tree growing in the middle of the road? He liked to write as if he knew the answers to those kinds of questions, as if he was born there in fact, or from the viewpoint of the corner grocer or an illegitimate child raised by the minister and his wife, or in the voice of the town cripple. The title of his book of essays and lectures on poetry is *The Triggering Town*. It's a pleasure to read, and the title chapter is filled with ideas for ways of looking at a town that can be used as writing exercises.

The importance of place is also discussed at length by the poet and novelist Margaret Atwood in her book *Survival: A Thematic Guide to Canadian Literature*. She studied the writing of her native Canada and compared it to that of the United States. She found that the concerns of Canadian writers seemed to arise out of their preoccupation with the landscape of that country, the harsh winters and wild open spaces. Survival, victimization, terror of nature, desolation, solitude, destruction, and courage are a few of the themes Atwood found Canadian writers to hold in common. Compared to American writers, Canadians explored these themes more frequently, reflecting what she calls "a national habit of mind." For Americans, Atwood says, this habit of mind often involves the idea of "the frontier," and "the journey." We tend to see all aspects of our lives this way, even our relationships. Wendell Berry has written a book called *The Country of Marriage,* in which he sees marriage as a new territory for exploration and discovery. The title poem of David Bottoms's third book, *In a U-Haul North of Damascus,* is about a man whose recent divorce compels him to travel across the country as a way of understanding what he's been through. (We've included this poem in "Twenty-Minute Writing Exercises" in the last section.)

In the Woody Allen film, "Annie Hall," the character grows up in an apartment on Coney Island under a roller coaster in an amusement park. The character becomes a stand-up comic, much like Allen himself. We can see how growing up under that roller coaster affected the comic's sensibilities. We see it in his strange brand of absurd, neurotic humor, hear it in the rhythms of his language and the timing of his jokes. How do your surroundings influence your poetry? Do you write in long, sweeping vistas, or are your poems like tall buildings, squat houses, ornate churches? What do your thoughts look like, your feelings? You may find surprising correspondences between your poems and where you live — or you may not yet have let your surroundings into your work.

Gary Snyder, Robert Hass, and Gary Young, among others, all write about California. The place moves them, and moves with them, making its way into their poetry. Here's a poem by Gary Young:

OUR LIFE IN CALIFORNIA

Near San Ardo the grasses tremble
and oak trees bend to the south against a constant wind.
Here our faith is tested
by the air that passes us ceaselessly
and takes each lost breath as we stumble through the hills.
The monotony of breathing, like our heartbeat,
is not the reassuring monotony
of the hills stacked row upon row
beyond our bearing and our ken.
The sun moves with the wind and will be gone,
but there is another light
coming from below, casting trees from the shadows.
There is a shadow beneath me
which moves as I move,
and the tracks I leave in the fragile grass
know more than I know of my duty here,
my worth and my chance.

Places leave their mark on us, and Young adds that we also leave our mark on them, even if it's only in the form of footprints. With the use of the words "we" and "our," Young creates a generous feeling of inclusiveness. We see ourselves as a group connected both *by* a place as well as *to* a place. It's interesting to compare Robert Winner's "six-story desert-like apartment buildings" to Young's "hills stacked row upon row." Whereas Winner describes the Bronx in the language of nature, Young appropriates the language of the city in his description of the natural world.

A *New Geography of Poets*, published by University of Arkansas Press, is a gathering of poets from all over America, presented by the region in which they live. Who are the poets in your area? How are you different; what sets you apart? How are you alike; what kinds of things specific to the place where you live unite you? These questions may form the basis for an exploration of what it means to be a poet in a particular place. Coupled with your own childhood landscapes, the place where you find yourself now may reveal itself to you in surprising ways. The writer's journey is both inward and outward. The poems we record along the way are the traces we leave, the tracks laid down for others to follow.

IDEAS FOR WRITING

1. How does growing up or living near the ocean, in the desert, in a small town or a large city influence your writing? Is life sparse or abundant, brilliant with color or subtly shaded? Is the animal life around you tame or wild? Is there an obvious change of seasons? Is the population large or small, working class or wealthy? Do you live near a factory, a river, a shopping mall, a nightclub, a school, or a graveyard? What's next door, down the street, around the corner? Write a poem about where you live as if you're writing to someone who's never been there. Use place names and street names, the names of neighborhoods, neighbors, and friends. Be detailed and specific.

2. In "The Palms," Smith begins with a sort of cinematic overview. Write a poem about some journey you took in the past—a road trip, hike, business trip, family vacation. Describe the particular place where you stopped off, broke down, or visited. Try to make the scene evocative of whatever your mood was at the time. At the end of the poem, see if you can do what Smith does—zoom in for a closeup.

3. Read C. K. Williams's poem "From My Window" in *Tar* or in his *Selected Poems,* and write your own poem describing a scene outside your own window. Do this even if your window faces a brick wall or a boring landscape; use your imagination to make it interesting.

4. Joyce Carol Oates has a short story titled, "Where Are You Going, Where Have You Been?" Make a list of all the places you've traveled to that you can remember with any vividness; make a second list of places where you'd like to go. Now brainstorm images—remembered or imagined—for these places. (Your images for Paris might include snow on iron benches in the Tuilleries, cats in the cemetery at Père Lachaise, croissants piled in a basket on a cafe table.) Write a poem that includes some of the places you've been, and at least one place you haven't. Find a common thread to connect the past and future: an emotion, a desire, a particular person.

5. Describe the house/apartment/trailer/condo/orphanage you spent time in as a child. If you lived in many places, pick the one that feels most alive with memories, images, emotions. In your poem, try to explain what that place meant to you at that time of your life; what were the discoveries you made there, what difficulties did you encounter?

6. Most of us, as children, had a secret hiding place or a favorite spot to get away from our families and our ordinary lives. It might have been a spot in the woods, a fort in the yard or basement, or the roof of the house. Write about your place and, if possible, a particular event/incident you recall that made you seek it out.

7. Take a two-hour field trip to someplace nearby, and stay there with your notebook recording images and impressions. Some possibilities: a hotel lobby; a cafe or restaurant; a woods; a laundromat; the beach. Make it someplace you haven't seen before, or at least haven't seen from the particular vantage point you choose. In a poem, recreate that place for someone else. Read

Galway Kinnell's poem "The Avenue Bearing the Initial of
Christ Into the New World," about Avenue C in New York City,
reprinted in his Pulitzer Prize-winning *Selected Poems.*

8. Brainstorm a list of words you identify with the city: skyscraper,
   crosswalk, asphalt, balcony, dumpster. Then make another list of
   words that are often used to describe the natural world: clouds,
   columbine, riverbed, granite. Write a descriptive poem about the
   city using words from your natural world word list, or a poem
   about the country using your city word list. Remember the
   poems by Winner and Young. Mixing things up like this will
   often spark fresh ideas and interesting language.

THE POET'S CRAFT

Images

Images haunt. There is a whole mythology built on this fact: Cezanne painting till his eyes bled, Wordsworth wandering the Lake Country hills in an impassioned daze. Blake describes it very well, and so did a colleague of Tu Fu who said to him, "It is like being alive twice." Images are not quite ideas, they are stiller than that, with less implications outside themselves. And they are not myth, they do not have that explanatory power; they are nearer to pure story. Nor are they always metaphors; they do not say this is that, they say this is.

—Robert Hass,
Twentieth Century Pleasures

We are all haunted by images, both light and dark. You might remember the smell of honeysuckle, or your father's cologne. A day in your childhood comes back, every detail sharp and precise, and you hear a shallow creek running over the rocks, your dog snuffling in wet leaves, your friend's voice calling you. You can still see the face of your dead aunt, or cousin, can taste the meal you choked down after the funeral. Frances Mayes, in *The Discovery of Poetry*, says that images are closely linked to memory, that in fact many of our memories consist of images. That partly explains why they're so powerful, why we respond to them in a much more visceral way than we do to generalized abstractions.

What, exactly, is an image? For most people, "image" carries the meaning of a visual picture, and it's true that many images are visual. Put simply, though, an image in poetry is language that calls up a physical sensation, appealing to us at the level of any of our five senses. Images may be *literal*: the red kitchen chair in a dim corner of the room; the gritty wet sand under her bare feet. Or they may be *figurative*, departing from the actual and stating or implying a comparison: the chair, red and shiny as fingernail polish; the armies of sand grains advancing across the wood floor of the beach house.

Think of going to the movies, how at first you are aware of yourself, sitting in a darkened theater, watching people and objects moving around on a screen. You are aware of the person sitting next to you, the walls or ceiling of the theater in your peripheral vision. Then a shift occurs and the world outside the screen falls away and you fall into the movie, aware of nothing but its world of story, emotions, images. And sometimes, an even stranger occurrence: the actor on screen lights a cigarette or pours a glass of wine and for an instant, the scent of smoke or grapes is in the air. Some synapse in your brain has been nudged and produces the memory of the aroma. Magic. That's what an image should do, produce a bit of magic, a reality so real it is "like being alive twice."

We all have our favorite sense. If you ask several people to describe coffee, one person might describe its smell, another its color, another its taste or the sound of beans being ground. Poets need to keep all five senses—and possibly a few more—on continual alert, ready to translate the world through their bodies, to reinvent it in language. Images are a kind of energy, moving from outside to inside and back, over and over, a continual exchange. You take a walk outside after the first snowfall of the season, fill your eyes with the dazzling surfaces of the fields and your lungs with the sharp pure air. Your boots sink in, crunching down to the frozen earth, and when you return to the cabin the warmth feels like a pair of gloved hands placed on your cold ears. You sit down and write about the snow. Miles away and years later, someone—a reader—closes her eyes and experiences it.

Images are seductive in themselves, but they're not merely scenery, or shouldn't be. An image, when it's doing its full work, can direct a reader toward some insight, bring a poem to an emotional pitch, embody an idea. Take a look at the following poem by T. R. Hummer, which unfolds in a succession of carefully chosen images.

WHERE YOU GO WHEN SHE SLEEPS

What is it when a woman sleeps, her head bright
In your lap, in your hands, her breath easy now as though it had
    never been
Anything else, and you know she is dreaming, her eyelids
Jerk, but she is not troubled, it is a dream
That does not include you, but you are not troubled either,
It is too good to hold her while she sleeps, her hair falling
Richly on your hands, shining like metal, a color
That when you think of it you cannot name, as though it has just
Come into existence, dragging you into the world in the wake
Of its creation, out of whatever vacuum you were in before,
And you are like the boy you heard of once who fell
Into a silo full of oats, the silo emptying from below, oats
At the top swirling in a gold whirlpool, a bright eddy of grain, the boy,
You imagine, leaning over the edge to see it, the noon sun breaking
Into the center of the circle he watches, hot on his back, burning
And he forgets his father's warning, stands on the edge, looks down,
The grain spinning, dizzy, and when he falls his arms go out, too thin
For wings, and he hears his father's cry somewhere, but is gone
Already, down in a gold sea, spun deep in the heart of the silo,
And when they find him, his mouth, his throat, his lungs
Full of the gold that took him, he lies still, not seeing the world
Through his body but through the deep rush of the grain
Where he has gone and can never come back, though they drag him
Out, his father's tears bright on both their faces, the farmhands
Standing by blank and amazed—you touch that unnamable
Color in her hair and you are gone into what is not fear or joy
But a whirling of sunlight and water and air full of shining dust
That takes you, a dream that is not of you but will let you
Into itself if you love enough, and will not, will never let you go.

    The speaker here is fascinated by the color of the woman's hair and overwhelmed by his love for her. He shows her to us, letting us observe her closely: her bright head in his lap, her easy breathing, the jerking of her eyelids. These literal images give way to figurative ones as he articulates his feelings: her hair is briefly "like metal," and then—in the long, wonderfully imagined description that follows—he compares himself to a boy falling into a silo. "Falling in love" is a familiar way of thinking about that dizzying rush of emotion; Hummer's image of falling into a silo full of oats, though, makes the reader *experience* that rush in a way that feels true, and yet new. Notice how he deepens his imagery by using specific, physical details: "swirling in a gold whirlpool" is a vivid visual image, while the noon sun "hot on his back, burning" is an image that is tactile—we can feel the sun, imagine ourselves falling "down in a gold sea, spun deep in the heart of the silo." Everything in the poem becomes connected, merges: the speaker of the poem is like the boy, the woman's hair is like the oats, the oats are like love. The image of the silo is both fascinating and frightening; love is both dream and nightmare, a sort of death which is terrible but also beautiful. Also notice that the whole poem is in the form of a question: "What is it . . . " The poet never really answers his question (Richard Hugo once said, "Never ask a question you can answer") but we know that Hummer is asking, "What is it like to fall in love?"

The poet enlivens his images with the use of color: "gold whirlpool," "gold sea," "full of the gold that took him." Brightness, gold, and sunlight are everywhere. Like the love described, the poem won't let us go—in one long sentence it takes us into that whirling and shining. Now look at how another writer, Gary Soto, uses color in this poem about young love.

ORANGES

The first time I walked
With a girl, I was twelve,
Cold, and weighted down
With two oranges in my jacket.
December. Frost cracking
Beneath my steps, my breath
Before me, then gone,
As I walked toward

Her house, the one whose
Porchlight burned yellow
Night and day, in any weather.
A dog barked at me, until
She came out, pulling
At her gloves, face bright
With rouge. I smiled.
Touched her shoulder, and led
Her across the street, across
A used car lot and a line
Of newly planted trees,
Until we were breathing
Before a drugstore. We
Entered, the tiny bell
Bringing a saleslady
Down a narrow aisle of goods.
I turned to the candies
Tiered like bleachers,
And asked what she wanted —
Light in her eyes, a smile
Starting at the corners
Of her mouth. I fingered
A nickel in my pocket,
And when she lifted a chocolate
That cost a dime I didn't say anything.
I took the nickel from
My pocket, then an orange,
And set them quietly on
The counter. When I looked up,
The lady's eyes met mine,
And held them, knowing
Very well what it was
About.
      Outside,
A few cars hissing past,
Fog hanging like old
Coats between the trees.
I took my girl's hand
In mine for two blocks,

Then released it to let
Her unwrap the chocolate.
I peeled my orange
That was so bright against
The gray of December
That, from some distance,
Someone might have thought
I was making a fire in my hands.

Knowing a little about how colors work together makes this poem and its last image even more impressive. Artists have used this trick: adding a bit of red to green to make the green appear brighter. Soto sets his orange against a gray sky. Using the color gray as a backdrop makes the orange brighter, larger, wilder, more like the fire he likens it to with words. Also notice the other colors and references to light used throughout the poem: the porchlight that burns yellow, the girl's face "bright with rouge," and the light in her eyes that precedes the fire in his hands, all carefully chosen to create a feeling of unity. Each of these specifics works toward animating that last incendiary image.

In his poem "Ghost," Robert Lowell wrote, "You cannot turn your back upon a dream, / for phantoms have their reasons when they come." The same could be said of images that haunt us, especially those which we work hardest to repress and that return to us unwanted and unbidden. In this poem by Marie Howe, the narrator is haunted by images of her younger sister being molested:

HOW MANY TIMES

No matter how many times I try I can't stop my father
from walking into my sister's room

and I can't see any better, leaning from here to look
in his eyes. It's dark in the hall

and everyone's sleeping. This is the past
where everything is perfect already and nothing changes,

where the water glass falls to the bathroom floor
and bounces once before breaking.

Nothing. Not the small sound my sister makes, turning
over, not the thump of the dog's tail

when he opens one eye to see him stumbling back to bed
still drunk, a little bewildered.

This is exactly as I knew it would be.
And if I whisper her name, hissing a warning,

I've been doing that for years now, and still the dog
startles and growls until he sees

it's our father, and still the door opens, and she
makes that small *oh* turning over.

As we've said, images aren't always primarily visual. This is a poem
in which the narrator's vision is in fact quite murky, even blocked.
She enlists the aid of the dog to help her see what she can't bear to
see. What she remembers more vividly is mostly auditory, the sounds
of the past: the water glass falling, the dog's tail thumping, a whisper,
a hiss, a growl, and then that heartbreaking "small *oh. . .* " Even the
absence of sound is important to this poem. These vivid images
enable us to feel the helplessness and vulnerability of the sister.

Images are the rendering of your bodily experience in the world;
without them, your poems are going to risk being vague and imprecise, and they will fail to convey much to a reader. The more you
practice with imagery—recording it in as much vivid detail as you
can—the more likely it is that your poetry will *become* an experience
for the reader, rather than simply talk *about* an experience. We are
surrounded by images daily. Pay attention to those images, and use
them to make your poems.

IDEAS FOR WRITING

1. What images obsess you? What do you think about when you are daydreaming? What kinds of images do you find yourself returning to or seeking out for comfort? What object, person, place, picture could you look at for hours and not get bored? Look at one of your obsessive pictures and describe it intimately. Do it in prose, quickly; don't worry about making it a poem yet. Then, contrast it with an image that you repress continually, that you really fight with. Describe that second image just as closely. Once you've done that, try joining the two images; mingle them as Hummer does in his poem, and see what happens.

2. Keep an image notebook for at least a month. Jot down the sights, sounds, tastes, smells and sensations of your life. These are good seeds for future poems; take an image you've noted and try to expand it with lots of descriptions, and with your ideas and feelings about that image.

3. Describe a pair of shoes in such a way that a reader will think of death. Do not mention death in the poem.

4. Write a poem composed primarily of auditory images.

5. It is said that our sense of smell is the most primitive, that a scent can take us back instantly into a memory. Jot down some smells that are appealing to you. For each one, describe the memory or experience associated with that smell, making sure you bring in the other senses in your description. Write a poem for each smell. For starters, you might title each poem with the triggering smell: "Roses," "Chanel No. 5," "Garlic," etc. Do the same for smells that you particularly dislike.

6. Take an image from a film, something that impressed itself on your memory, and write about it. Describe the image or scene and then try to talk about why it made such an impression.

7. Describe a painting or photograph (not an abstract one, but something that pictures people or objects) as though the scene is really happening; animate it with movement, speech, story.

Simile and Metaphor

Imagine a literal world, in which nothing was ever seen in terms of anything else. Falling blossoms wouldn't remind you of snow. A dancer's sensuous grace wouldn't resemble the movements of a lover; the shape of a cloud would never suggest a horse or a sailing ship. If such a world were possible, it would be a severely impoverished one.

In fact, we live in a figurative world; our language and our thinking, our very perceptions, are metaphoric. We continually make comparisons and connections, often without even realizing that we are doing so, so comfortable are we with seeing in this way. Contrary to what you might think if you are beginning to study the craft of poetry, the use of figurative language isn't a new skill; it's one you already know. The trouble is that most of the figures in our language are so common and have been heard so often that they're virtually useless for poetry, which deals not in clichéd, worn-out expressions but in surprising ones that reveal new connections or cast a different angle of light on an idea or experience. (There, we've just resorted to figurative language—"cast a different angle of light"—to explain what we mean.) "Love is a rose" would not be high on our list as a poetic metaphor, but try "In my book love is darker / than cola. It can burn / a hole clean through you," from C. D. Wright, or Charles Bukowski's "Love is a dog from hell." Good metaphors and similes make connections that deepen, expand, and energize; they stimulate the imagination. Once, perhaps, to say "she sticks to him like glue" was fresh and interesting, but now it's a simile that, if it turns up in your poem, should be sent to the Toxic Language Dump—a place we've invented for all those expressions that are deadly for the art. The Toxic Language Dump is a place you should get familiar with as a writer. One difference between good and not-so-good poets is that the good ones recognize when they've written stuff that deserves to be dumped, and load up the truck. The not-so-good poets leave it in. There's a line at the end of Norman Dubie's "The Funeral," about the death of an aunt, that has always haunted us: "The cancer ate her like horse piss eats deep snow." That's a memorable image, one so apt and effective it resonates years after reading it.

But using figurative language in poetry is more than finding a startling simile or metaphor that grabs your reader. Look at a poem by Sharon Olds, who we're convinced has a machine in her basement which operates day and night generating similes. Along with her odd line breaks and often intense emotional subject matter, Olds's prodigious use of similes immediately stands out as characteristic of her style. Here's a poem from her first book, *Satan Says*:

FEARED DROWNED

Suddenly nobody knows where you are,
your suit black as seaweed, your bearded
head slick as a seal's.

Somebody watches the kids. I walk down the
edge of the water, clutching the towel
like a widow's shawl around me.

None of the swimmers is just right.
Too short, too heavy, clean-shaven,
they rise out of the surf, the water
rushing down their shoulders.

Rocks stick out near shore like heads.
Kelp snakes in like a shed black suit
and I cannot find you.

My stomach begins to contract as if to
vomit salt water

when up the sand toward me comes
a man who looks very much like you,
his beard matted like beach grass, his suit
dark as a wet shell against his body.

Coming closer, he turns out
to be you—or nearly.
Once you lose someone it is never exactly
the same person who comes back.

Look carefully at the similes in this poem. What if Olds had written, in the second line, "your suit black as burnt toast," or "black as a
cockroach's back"? Such a radical alteration would, of course,
wrench the poem in another direction, taking us away from its central concern: the speaker's fear that her companion might have
drowned. The similes here reinforce her anxiety, help us as readers
identify with it. They also set the scene vividly: we can see exactly
how this woman walks along the edge of the water "clutching the
towel like a widow's shawl." Had she said only "shawl," we'd still get
a clear picture, but imagining the widow's shawl lets us experience
her emotional state as well. Strong similes and metaphors are integral
to a poem's meaning; they aren't merely clever comparisons tacked
on. Figurative language is a way to deepen and intensify the themes
and concerns of your work.

    After you've written a draft of a poem, at some point you might want
to take a look at how you've handled that figurative level of language.
Perhaps you've stuck to the strictly literal, and the associations of the
poem could be expanded with the use of simile or metaphor. Or you
might have chosen a comparison that takes the poem in the wrong
direction—towards a meaning you didn't intend, or towards a humor-
ous tone when you were trying for something serious. Explore the implications of your language, too, to see what you've said. Was that disas-
trous love relationship really like a head-on collision, or was it more like
jumping from a plane with a defective parachute? Both imply damage—but in the first case you've probably both ended up with broken
glass all over you, while in the second, you're the one who's crashed.

    Another thing about the figurative: it gives you access to words and
images that wouldn't be there otherwise. Take the above example: in

the first case you might use words like highway, headlights, metal, screech, crush. In the second, you'd have a different group of words: wind, space, fall, ripcord, and the like. Take advantage of the vocabulary that accompanies your figure; exploit it for its possibilities, so it adds energy and depth to your poem.

We'd like to mention a couple of other things we admire in "Feared Drowned." At the end of the poem, the "you," previously the speaker's husband or lover, changes. Now the "you" is anyone, and the reader is included in that "you." "Once you lose someone" lifts the poem from a private experience to a shared one, since all of us have lost someone in one way or another. Even to imagine losing someone, Olds seems to say, changes how we see them; now we're aware of the possibility of loss. We were also struck by some of the rhythms in the poem; read aloud lines like "Too short, too heavy, clean-shaven" to hear the insistence in those words: TOO SHORT, TOO HEAvy, CLEAN SHAVE-en. She seems to be saying to herself, NOT YOU, NOT YOU, NOT YOU as her panic builds; the missing person is not one of the swimmers. Or listen to "Kelp snakes in like a shed black suit." Olds's simile machine also knows how to sing.

Simile and metaphor are often distinguished from each other with the explanation that similes use "like," "as," or some other connector, while metaphors remove it and say simply that one thing *is* another. "That child acts like an angel" becomes simply, "that child is an angel." But metaphors aren't always contained within poems in discrete bits; often, entire poems work on a metaphoric level. This is one of the pleasures of both reading and writing poems: the recasting of one thing in terms of another, the revelation of the ways outwardly different experiences can be seen to have a similar core. In "Feared Drowned," Olds makes a particular experience a metaphor for loss, and explicitly asks us to consider our own losses in the last two lines.

The next two poems by Jack Gilbert talk about the death of his wife, Michiko.

FINDING SOMETHING

I say moon is horses in the tempered dark,
because horse is the closest I can get to it.
I sit on the terrace of this worn villa the king's

telegrapher built on the mountain that looks down
on a blue sea and the small white ferry
that crosses slowly to the next island each noon.
Michiko is dying in the house behind me,
the long windows open so I can hear
the faint sound she will make when she wants
watermelon to suck or so I can take her
to a bucket in the corner of the high-ceilinged room
which is the best we can do for a chamber pot.
She will lean against my leg as she sits
so as not to fall over in her weakness.
How strange and fine to get so near to it.
The arches of her feet are like voices
of children calling in the grove of lemon trees,
where my heart is as helpless as crushed birds.

The metaphor that opens this poem, and the similes that close it, are magical, almost surreal. Perhaps the horses are meant to suggest a journey—the narrator's wife is on her way to death. The dark is "tempered," the way a metal like steel is tempered, brought to the proper hardness by being heated and suddenly cooled; again, there's the resonance with dying, the cooling of the body as heat and energy go out of it. After this evocative beginning, the poet goes on to describe the scene and Michiko's suffering. Grief and beauty are mingled: "How strange and fine to get so near to it," he says, and then compares the arches of his wife's feet to the voices of children. Is he imaginatively led to the children by gazing at her feet, the way one passes under the arch of a doorway? He is called to her and yet away from her, to the lemon trees; and his heart is "helpless as crushed birds." A reader sees and feels those crushed birds, and the narrator's broken heart, simultaneously. Inner and outer landscape have meshed.

The next poem deals with the aftermath of death. To describe how one goes on after grief, Gilbert uses the image of carrying a box. We all understand grief as heaviness; and in fact, the word for grief comes from the Latin *gravis*, meaning weighty, sad. The simile is introduced in the first line and then sustained and extended throughout the poem, to concretely and precisely evoke how the process of grieving feels from one day to the next.

MICHIKO DEAD

He manages like somebody carrying a box
that is too heavy, first with his arms
underneath. When their strength gives out,
he moves the hands forward, hooking them
on the corners, pulling the weight against
his chest. He moves his thumbs slightly
when the fingers begin to tire, and it makes
different muscles take over. Afterward,
he carries it on his shoulder, until the blood
drains out of the arm that is stretched up
to steady the box and the arm goes numb. But now
the man can hold underneath again, so that
he can go on without ever putting the box down.

The heart is never finished with grief; that's the assertion of the poem. Though the burden is "too heavy," we manage it. A box is an apt image; we might think of a coffin, or a box of ashes. A heavy box might be filled with all our memories of someone, of the time we spent with them. The box in the poem is painful to carry, yet precious to the man who cannot, or will not, put it down.

Many poems don't make their comparisons explicit, the way this one does. A poem may consist entirely of literal images, but they may well resonate with metaphorical meaning. In "Finding Something," a ferry crosses the water—a seemingly literal description of what the narrator sees, but one that also recalls Greek mythology, in which the souls of the dead were ferried across the rivers of the underworld. Every day the white ferry travels "to the next island"; one day, Michiko's soul will be ferried away.

In this poem by Katha Pollitt, archaeology is a metaphor for writing poetry; but without the epigraph, we'd still know that she was referring to more than digging up bones and artifacts. The process described could serve for any creative activity that demands patient and loving attention.

ARCHAEOLOGY

"Our real poems are already in us
and all we can do is dig."
—Jonathan Galassi

You knew the odds on failure from the start,
that morning you first saw, or thought you saw,
beneath the heatstruck plains of a second-rate country
the outline of buried cities. A thousand to one
you'd turn up nothing more than the rubbish heap
of a poor Near Eastern backwater:
a few chipped beads,
splinters of glass and pottery, broken tablets
whose secret lore, laboriously deciphered,
would prove to be only a collection of ancient grocery lists.
Still, the train moved away from the station without you.

How many lives ago
was that? How many choices?
Now that you've got your bushelful of shards
do you say, *give me back my years*
or wrap yourself in the distant
glitter of desert stars,
telling yourself it was foolish after all
to have dreamed of uncovering
some fluent vessel, the bronze head of a god?
Pack up your fragments. Let the simoom
flatten the digging site. Now come
the passionate midnights in the museum basement
when out of that random rubble you'll invent
the dusty market smelling of sheep and spices,
streets, palmy gardens, courtyards set with wells
to which, in the blue of evening, one by one
come strong veiled women, bearing their perfect jars.

Pollitt imagines the poet as archaeologist. Poets know "the odds on failure" when they first imagine the not-yet-written poem, when they are first moved by that mysterious impulse to articulate something. In spite of the difficulties of making a good poem, and the real possibility that the results will be unsatisfactory, poets take on the task. A life committed to that task, Pollitt suggests, has its price. But in the end, it's clearly worth it: out of that "random rubble" something wonderful can be made. She takes advantage of the possibilities of language associated with her metaphor: "heatstruck plains," "splinters of glass and pottery," "simoom," "palmy gardens." Extending your similes and metaphors in this manner, rather than simply sprinkling them through your poems, can help you to explore the implications of your ideas and your images. Notice that "Archaeology" not only uses a central metaphor, but finds within it parallels for each step of the process—those "passionate midnights" in the basement are a metaphor for the work of shaping the materials of a poem, writing and revising until the imagined world is fully formed. In developing your own figurative images, don't worry if your language is clumsy or confusing at first. Just have patience, and keep digging.

IDEAS FOR WRITING

1. Here are a few similes we like. After reading them, complete the unfinished ones; try for something unexpected.

> Her breasts like white wolves' heads
> sway and snarl.
> > —Sharon Olds

> The baled wheat scattered
> everywhere like missing coffins
> > —Carolyn Forché

> Her body is not so white as
> anemone petals nor so smooth—nor
> so remote a thing.
>
> > —William Carlos Williams

> Loneliness spreading
> fast like a gas fire
> —Frances Mayes

> A gull is locked like a ghost in the blue attic of heaven.
> —Charles Wright

tired as . . .
hot as . . .
waves unfurled like . . .
after the shelling, the town looked as if . . .
disgusting as . . .
the child trembled like . . .
the airplane rose like a . . .
black as . . .
he entered the room like . . .
their lovemaking was like . . .

2. There's an old joke that goes, "Your teeth are like stars. They come out at night." The second sentence reverses our expectations of "like stars." In a poem by Margaret Atwood, a similar reversal occurs. The first lines read: "You fit into me / like a hook into an eye." Some clothes are held together by hook and eye—a small metal catch that hooks onto a loop, or an eye. The next lines, however, change the cozy image into something much more ominous: "a fish hook / an open eye." See if you can dream up some similes that change direction like this and surprise a reader's expectations of where they're headed.

3. Write a poem about a disturbing experience, using lots of unified similes, taking "Feared Drowned" as a model. Then write a second poem on the same experience, only using as many *different* similes as possible for what the experience was like; that is, keep changing the comparisons: "It was like . . . Or else it was like . . . "

4. Describe an activity—cleaning the house, fishing, painting a picture, bathing a child, dancing, cooking a meal—which could serve as a metaphor for your life, for how you are in the world.

5. Using "Archaeology" as a model, think about what the process of writing a poem is like for you: building a bridge? falling off a cliff? baking bread? taking an ocean voyage? Once you've chosen the metaphor for your creative process, make a list of vocabulary you might use, specific to that metaphor. Then write the poem, trying to work in the most interesting words.

6. Write a brief seven-to-ten-line poem with an abstract title: Loneliness, Fear, Desire, Ecstasy, Greed, Suffering, Pleasure. Make the poem a metaphor for the title, without using the abstraction in the poem.

7. Write a "negative simile" poem: "It wasn't like _____, or _____ . . ."

8. Write a poem using a simile or metaphor which goes on for at least five lines.

9. Find a poem you wrote some time ago and add at least three similes or metaphors to it.

The Music of the Line

A first thought is that the line is a unit *to work in . . .*
—Sandra McPherson

The line, when a poem is alive in its sound, measures:
it is a proposal about listening.
—Robert Hass,
Twentieth Century Pleasures

Most people who are beginning to write poetry are confused about line breaks. They wonder what the difference is between a poem and "chopped-up prose." They arrange their thoughts in lines without much sense of why they are doing so, beyond the hope that if what they write *looks* like a poem, it will mysteriously become one. We think McPherson's comment is a good place to begin thinking about the line: not as something language is "broken" into, but a method of making a poem—a line by line, brick by brick construction. Ellen Bryant Voigt made a similar statement at the Bread Loaf Writers Conference one year, asking the participants in a workshop, "Do you break your poems *into* lines, or compose *by* the line?" When you write, you may indeed find yourself at first getting your thoughts out in prose, and then trying to make a poem from that. Even so, we feel that this concept of the line as a unit of composition is an important one. At some point, if you want to make memorable poems, you'll need to get a feel for the line, for what it does when it is very short, very long, and every place in between; you'll need to be able to test its weight and heft according to the rhythms of the language you've strung along it; and you'll want to use it to create tension or relaxation, to emphasize words, to speed up or slow down your reader's eye, to fulfill or thwart expectations. These are the advantages of the skillfully used line, and like any other aspect of craft, such skill comes from practice.

There are no real rules for line breaks. Give the same paragraph of prose to five poets, and each might break it into interesting lines; but their versions probably won't be identical. There's often no single correct way to do it. Instead, think of line breaks as effects; learn the different effects you can achieve, and then decide which you want. At first you'll feel very much at sea, but gradually, by experimenting and listening, and by noticing how line works for other writers, you'll begin to gain a sense of control.

Denise Levertov says that the pause at the end of a line is equal to a half-comma. The reader's eye and ear, having taken in the words and rhythms of the line, get a brief respite before going on to the next. In other words, there's a momentary *silence*; and as musicians know, silence is an integral part of the music. A line break is not just a pause in the action of the poem; it's very much a part of it. In a piece of music, the silence is notated by a rest, which tells the performer how long the silence lasts. Think of line breaks as rests in the music of your poem, and stanza breaks as longer rests. Meanwhile, of course, there's the line itself, with its flowing or agitated rhythms, its own pauses within it that are the result of commas, periods, dashes—anything that interrupts the words. Poets need to tune their ears as finely as musicians; that's why reading poems aloud is a good idea, including your own poems as you write them.

You need not be familiar with meter to gain an appreciation for the rhythms of writers' lines, and to begin to work with this principle yourself. All you need to do is to be able to hear the inflections of the language—which parts of words get a stress, a little push, when you say them aloud. Say the word "lily." You should hear it as a *stressed* syllable, followed by an unstressed one (also called a *slack* syllable):

LIL-y. Or try "forget": for-GET. Or how about AR-i-a, and in-FIN-i-ty, and BLACK-ber-ry.

Here are the opening lines from a poem by Seamus Heaney, "Mother of the Groom":

> What she remembers
> Is his glistening back
> In the bath, his small boots
> In the ring of boots at her feet.

Read it aloud to yourself. You should hear it this way:

> WHAT she reMEMbers
> Is his GLIStening BACK
> In the BATH, his SMALL BOOTS
> In the RING of BOOTS at her FEET.

This kind of reading is not always precise; you may pronounce some words differently than other people, or feel that some syllables seem to want a half-stress when placed next to those more strongly stressed. In the example above, you might not hear the word "What" in the first line as stressed; the poem could be read either way. Poetry lacks the more sophisticated notational system used for music; poets can only suggest certain intonations and ways of speaking. It's impossible to reproduce the nuances of the human voice on the page. That's why it's especially important to pay attention to the tools we do have, to become aware of the sounds of language and begin to work with them—both in your choice of words, and how you organize those words into lines that are meaningful—not only in what they say, but how they say it.

Before we go on, a couple of definitions will be helpful. An *end-stopped* line means just that: at the end of the line, there's a period that tells you to stop, or a semicolon, or a comma that makes you pause. The fourth line of "Mother of the Groom" is end-stopped. When a line is *enjambed*, it simply runs on to the next one, as the first three lines of the poem do. If a sentence goes on for several lines, the enjambment makes for a feeling of forward motion; when you get to the period that ends both the sentence and the line, you're going to have a momentary sense of completion, a release from tension. Take, for example, this well-known poem, by Gwendolyn Brooks:

WE REAL COOL

The Pool Players.
Seven at the Golden Shovel.

We real cool. We
Left school. We

Lurk late. We
Strike straight. We

Sing sin. We
Thin gin. We

Jazz June. We
Die soon.

If this poem were written in end-stopped lines, it would look like this:

We real cool.
We left school.

We lurk late.
We strike straight.

We sing sin.
We thin gin.

We jazz June.
We die soon.

Read these two versions aloud; you'll hear how the second one has lost its energy, how it lacks the syncopated feel Brooks gets from that "We" at the end of each line. In our rendition, the rhymes of late-straight, sin-gin, and June-soon sound heavy-handed and obvious. The end-stopped lines plod along; the last statement, which is now in the exact rhythm of the previous lines, no longer surprises. Brooks's

poem ends, not only with a different rhythm, but with the conspicu-
ous absence of that "We" we've come to expect at the end of the line,
an omission that serves to point up the absence of these bragging pool
players whose lives will be cut short.

Denise Levertov is a writer whose work is always carefully crafted,
always alert to the musical possibilities of the line. Here's one of her
poems, which deals with a kind of stasis, a waiting for inspiration, perhaps—the narrator feels trapped, frustrated, unable to get to the thing
that will release her into language.

WHERE IS THE ANGEL?

Where is the angel for me to wrestle?
No driving snow in the glass bubble,
but mild September.

Outside, the stark shadows
menace, and fling their huge arms about
unheard. I breathe

a tepid air, the blur
of asters, of brown fern and gold-dust
seems to murmur,

and that's what I hear, only that.
Such clear walls of curved glass:
I see the violent gesticulations

and feel—no, not nothing. But in this
gentle haze, nothing commensurate.
It is pleasant in here. History

mouths, volume turned off. A band of iron,
like they put round a split tree,
circles my heart. In here

it is pleasant, but when I open
my mouth to speak, I too
am soundless. Where is the angel

to wrestle with me and wound
not my thigh but my throat,
so curses and blessings flow storming out

and the glass shatters, and the iron sunders?

If you read this poem carefully, with your ears as well as your eyes, you'll hear Levertov's control of each line. Notice where the ends of sentences occur. In the first stanza, there's the opening question and the last line of the stanza. After that, though, we find only three lines end-stopped with periods. Two occur, not at the end of stanzas, but inside them: "and that's what I hear, only that" in the fourth stanza, and "gentle haze, nothing commensurate" in the fifth. Stanzas can be thought of as being either end-stopped or enjambed, too, in a sense; that is, if an end-stopped line occurs *before* the final line of the stanza, we still have that sense of tension, and want to read on. So Levertov keeps us moving through her poem all the way to its final line. Each stanza ends, not with the satisfaction of a stopping point, but in the middle of some idea the writer is pursuing. This makes the final question resonate with greater power, since it brings us to rest after a long wait. She's also set off the last line by itself, after sticking to a three-line stanza throughout the poem. Considering the fact that the narrator is still trapped at the end of the poem, still wondering where her angel could be, the departure of that single last line is significant—it's a vividly imagined breaking out, as the line breaks out from the stanza pattern, even though the event hasn't occurred.

The rhythms of certain lines also serve to intensify the contrasts in the poem. Levertov is working with two different states: the almost numb, dull space the narrator inhabits, and the imagined one outside her "glass bubble." So we get "driving snow" versus "mild September," "violent gesticulations" versus "gentle haze," "silence" versus "curses and blessings." But she also gives us the contrast more subtly, by setting up certain lines so that they reinforce her theme through rhythm. Look at the following:

> unHEARD. i BREATHE
> Such CLEAR WALLS of CURVED GLASS
> not my THIGH but my THROAT
> and the GLASS SHATters, and the IRon SUNders

In each case, the same rhythm is repeated in the line, so that we get it in parallel. Nothing storms out of these perfectly balanced lines. They're pleasant, as harmony is pleasant, but that's not what the narrator seeks. What she is after, she describes this way: "so curses and blessings flow storming out"; and the rhythm of that line gives us the rush of energy she'd like to experience.

A general principle of line breaks is that the word at the end of the line, and to a lesser extent at the beginning of it, stands out a bit more to the reader. You can see this working particularly strongly towards the end of Levertov's poem. When she describes "A band of iron, / like they put round a split tree," the opposition of "iron" and "tree" is made more obvious. The words at the ends of other lines are also significant ones. You can emphasize important ideas in your own poems the same way.

Levertov's poem is quiet, controlled; even when she uses enjambment, the poem *proceeds* rather than rushes headlong down the page. The rhythms are appropriate to the subject matter, and help to reinforce the tone and mood as well. Paul Monette's poem "Here," whose speaker is dealing with the loss of his lover, Roger, to AIDS, adopts a very different strategy.

HERE

everything extraneous has burned away
this is how burning feels in the fall
of the final year not like leaves in a blue
October but as if the skin were a paper lantern
full of trapped moths beating their fired wings
and yet I can lie on this hill just above you
a foot beside where I will lie myself
soon soon and for all the wrack and blubber
feel still how we were warriors when the
merest morning sun in the garden was a
kingdom after Room 1010 war is not all
death it turns out war is what little
thing you hold on to refugeed and far from home
oh sweetie will you please forgive me this
that every time I opened a box of anything
Glad Bags One-A-Days KINGSIZE was
the worst I'd think will you still be here
when the box is empty Rog Rog who will

> play boy with me now that I bucket with tears
> through it all when I'd cling beside you sobbing
> you'd shrug it off with the quietest *I'm still*
> *here* I have your watch in the top drawer
> which I don't dare wear yet help me please
> the boxes grocery home day after day
> the junk that keeps men spotless but it doesn't
> matter now how long they last or I
> the day has taken you with it and all
> there is now is burning dark the only green
> is up by the grave and this little thing
> of telling the hill I'm here oh I'm here

The poem is an outpouring that allows the reader no opportunity to stop and consider. Part of this clearly comes from Monette's decision to forgo conventional punctuation; lines that would normally be end-stopped, like the first one, now open into the rest of the poem. Even the last line lacks a period, so that we feel cast away from the final word "here" into the blankness of the page. The sentences run together and help us to experience the speaker's distraught state. Wordsworth once defined poetry as "emotion recollected in tranquility," but this poem expresses the white heat of immediate grief. The way that Monette breaks many of his lines adds to the visceral appeal of his language; we're made uncomfortable when words that usually go together are suddenly severed from each other, like adjectives and nouns ("blue / October"), articles and nouns ("the / merest morning sun," "a / kingdom"), when even verbs are split up ("Rog Rog who will / play boy with me now," "but it doesn't / matter now how long they last"). These and other line breaks cut across the normal flow of sentences and are disorienting at times, mimicking and recreating the powerful emotions the writer wishes to convey. Altering just a few lines will give you a sense of how the poem would change:

> feel still how we were warriors
> when the merest morning sun in the garden
> was a kingdom after Room 1010
> war is not all death it turns out

war is what little thing you hold on to
refugeed and far from home

While the above version might make the poem a bit clearer on a
first reading, it has lost some of the intensity and drive of the original.
Sometimes this is the choice you'll make in your own work; your
poem may need the line-by-line unfolding of clear statements or
images, so that each thing is presented before moving on. At other
times you'll want to experiment with creating the kind of tension and
dislocation you can achieve by such severe enjambment.

We haven't, so far, said anything about short lines versus long lines.
We read somewhere that short lines speed up the pace of a poem, but
we feel the opposite; we experience a poem in short lines as a more
gradual movement. Read a few such poems—William Carlos
Williams and Robert Creeley wrote many—and see what you think.
One thing we're certain of: the shorter the line (and the shorter the
poem), the tighter the language has to be. All that white space around
your words makes them really stand out. We're not suggesting that
you write badly and hope to disguise it in long lines; that can't be
done. But you might find it helpful to double- or even triple-space
your lines, and to shorten them, to catch any flawed language. Short
lines have another advantage, too: it's easier for you, as you're writing,
to hear their rhythms. Write a few short lines and practice saying
them out loud, so that you really hear the beats, the stressed and slack
syllables; then try longer ones. A poet who handles the very long line
beautifully, and is actually one of the few contemporary writers using
it, is C. K. Williams. You should also look at Allen Ginsberg's famous
poem "Howl," as well as his "Kaddish"; at Robinson Jeffers, who
wrote earlier in the twentieth century; and of course, read the poetry
of Walt Whitman. Line lengths, ultimately, are something you develop a knack for by fooling around with them. The same goes for using
stanzas, and for starting lines somewhere other than the left-hand
margin. As we said earlier, there are no real rules, only effects. Be
careful that you don't become so enamored of what a line break can
do that you begin using it as a clever trick, rather than a technique to
serve your poem.

IDEAS FOR WRITING

1. Take a draft of a poem and rewrite it in the following ways:
   very short lines
   very long lines
   some length in between
   in three-line stanzas
   in five-line stanzas
   You will probably find yourself changing some of the words as you try out the various versions, adding and deleting material.

2. Look at several of your poems. Is there a line length that seems characteristic of you? Or do you tend to mix up long and short lines in the same poem? The same goes for stanzas: do you tend to write in one block, or always to use four-line stanzas? If you find you have a pattern, write a poem that breaks it.

3. Write a poem that is an emotional outburst—of joy, anger, love—using a lot of enjambment, and few end-stopped lines. Play with breaking apart parts of language that normally go together.

4. Write a short nonsense poem, maximum five lines, in which you pay attention to the rhythms of each line rather than the logical meaning of the words. Read it aloud several times. When you know the rhythms well, and like how they fit together, try to substitute meaningful words in the exact same rhythms.

5. Break the prose below into lines three different ways, to make three different poems, and study the effects of each version. In judging the results, think about the following: which words have been emphasized in each version? How are you working with the sentence structure—when are you highlighting it, or undercutting it? Is there a tone or mood in the prose that one version seems to capture best?

   The cows stand under the trees in the wet grass, lifting their necks to pull leaves down. We slow the truck, pull over to the side of the road to watch them. How graceful they look, how

unlike themselves. We get out and lean on the fence. The
cows don't seem to notice we are there.

6. Choose a poet you admire, read at least one book of his or her
   work, and carefully study how this writer uses line and stanza.
   Then take a draft of one of your own poems, and redo the lines
   and stanzas as you imagine this writer would.

7. Take a short poem by William Carlos Williams such as "The
   Great Figure" or "The Red Wheelbarrow," and copy the rhythms
   of his lines exactly, substituting your own words.

8. Do the above for any poet you like, to sensitize your ear to the
   poet's rhythms, and your own.

Voice and Style

We convince by our presence.
> —Walt Whitman

I am a black woman poet and I sound like one.
> —Lucille Clifton

When we listen to a person speaking, we hear a particular music unlike any other. The stamp of someone's voice is as individual as a fingerprint; if we know someone well, we instantly recognize the tone, pitch, resonance of that voice whenever we encounter it. In poetry, the term *voice* has been used to describe that sense of a unique presence on the page — an unmistakable something that becomes the mark of a writer, a way of saying things that is the writer's own. This is usually what developing writers mean when they say they are trying to find their voice; some would argue that it wasn't lost to begin with, that we all have a voice already. But either way, this idea of a recognizable voice is an important one for writers. We struggle with the voices of the past, the poets who came before us, and we try to learn from them without sounding like them. We read contemporary writers and imitate their line breaks, or their similes, and worry that we shouldn't, that we'll only create bad reproductions instead of original works. We want a presence that convinces, one that engages and seduces a reader into the world of our poems, a voice a reader will want to listen to. When we fail to produce this voice, the poem fails. The reader laughs when we want her to cry, or turns away disinterestedly when we passionately want his attention. The poem doesn't communicate what we meant; the voice is garbled, confused, talking to itself.

In actual speech, we don't choose our voice. We grow up inheriting speech patterns and physical structures that largely determine how we sound. In poetry, we may write with a voice that is also determined by things beyond our control—an innate sense of language, early education, and previous exposure to other writers. But just as someone might go to a speech therapist to rid himself of a stutter, or erase a particular accent, writers can develop their voice so that it becomes a more flexible instrument to articulate their concerns. *Style* is really interchangeable with voice, in this sense, and it's useful to remember that style in a writer is revealed by the characteristic *choices* a writer makes. Beginning writers often sound remarkably alike, because they have the same limited range of choices; they haven't yet discovered a wider range. If you haven't done much reading or writing of poetry, you're going to make your choices based on a narrow sampling of what you know, which might range from the sappy clichés of greeting cards to some fuzzily-remembered poets from earlier centuries crammed down your throat in high school, to popular song lyrics. That is, you'll make choices by default—rather than from a rich storehouse of possibilities discovered through working and playing with language, and through reading. Writing and reading are the only ways to find your voice. It won't magically burst forth in your poems the next time you sit down to write, or the next; but little by little, as you become aware of more choices and begin to make them—consciously and unconsciously—your style will develop.

What are the choices a writer makes, that constitute a recognizable voice and style? If you're studying someone's style, just about every aspect of her poems is worth considering. Let's look at two by Lucille Clifton, to see what can be discovered about her presence on the page.

homage to my hips

these hips are big hips
they need space to
move around in.
they do not fit into little
petty places, these hips
are free hips.
they don't like to be held back.
these hips have never been enslaved,
they go where they want to go
they do what they want to do.
these hips are mighty hips.
these hips are magic hips.
i have known them
to put a spell on a man and
spin him like a top!

the women you are accustomed to

wearing that same black dress,
their lips and asses tight,
their bronzed hair set in perfect place;
these women gathered in my dream
to talk their usual talk,
their conversation spiked with the names
of avenues in France.

and when i asked them what the hell,
they shook their marble heads
and walked erect out of my sleep,
back into a town which knows
all there is to know
about the cold outside, while i relaxed
and thought of you,
your burning blood, your dancing tongue.

Does Clifton sound like a black woman poet? There's a reference to enslavement in the first poem, and both are about the female body.

Certainly, being a black woman poet has been one of Clifton's subjects. The sensuality and celebration of these poems are also characteristic of her work. Her poems tend to be short, to forgo capitals and
sometimes titles. They're small, but they tackle large subjects. They
want to connect; they're accessible, seemingly simple, but not simplistic. We hear a voice speaking directly, more conversational than
formal. The person Clifton creates on the page speaks with passion
and sometimes humor. This is a style that wants to collapse the distance between writer and reader, and between the poet and her
poem. Of course, two poems is a small sampling; Clifton doesn't
always write about her body, or about her own life, or in first person.
If you wanted to further analyze Clifton's style, you'd need to read
more of her work. (Her latest is *The Terrible Stories* from BOA
Editions.)

Doing a close analysis of any writer is a useful exercise that can
teach you a lot about why you may like or dislike the poems—why
they appeal to you, why they move you or make you cringe. Of
course, there's a mysterious element in poetry that seems to resist
intellectual analysis, and this is good. William Carlos Williams said,
"A poem is a machine made of words," and while it may be true that
each word contributes to the smooth functioning of a poem, there's
an organic and irreducible energy in a good poem that can't be logically accounted for. Call it the spark, the "blood-jet," as Sylvia Plath
did, or whatever you will; you can take the poem apart and you won't
find it. But from the standpoint of technique, you can learn from
studying the styles of other writers—and from stepping back to take a
good look at your own characteristic choices. Here's a list of things
you might want to consider.

1. Subject matter. Subject and style, content and form—they really
are inseparable. Still, poems are generally *about* something. Because
writers write out of their interests, their beliefs and obsessions, particular subjects often become part of how we recognize them. Whitman
wrote about the common mass of humanity, not the wealthy in their
drawing rooms; Robert Lowell's work began to seem radically different when he started producing pieces about his family; Anne Sexton

wrote about suicide and the body, Sylvia Plath about death and the true and false self. Sharon Olds, in each of her first three books, wrote poems about her father; the fourth was titled *The Father*, and every poem concerned him. C. K. Williams often takes the internal workings of his mind, or the dynamics of relationships, as his subject; his poems are frequently discursive and psychological. Is your own subject matter too narrow or too broad? What are your subjects? Are you exploring the material you feel compelled to tackle? Are there new subjects for poems that you haven't considered? Asking these questions of your work may lead you to new and deeper material.

2. Diction. Diction is word choice, the vocabulary of the poem. Some writers take what we'll call the high road—it's hard to get through their poems without a dictionary. (At least, we can't.) The high road is filled with long, Latinate words—"expectorate" instead of "spit," "indefatigable" instead of "untiring," and so on. In much modern and contemporary poetry, the tendency has been to move away from such diction, to try for the language of ordinary speech, heightened by careful crafting. Taking the high road is tricky, but some writers have done it successfully. The danger is that you'll sound pompous and overinflated; the danger of ordinary diction is that you'll sound ordinary. In any case, you'll want to look carefully at the words you've chosen. At what level do you want to pitch your poem? Who's speaking in the poem; would that person use the words you've chosen for her? Maybe you want to mix up different dictions and have several ways of speaking occurring in the same poem, as John Berryman did in his *Dream Songs*. Who do you imagine reading your poem? Besides these issues, there's the consideration of writing in the language of your time. Some student writers have baffled us by insisting that they do not mind sounding like Shakespeare or Shelley or someone else long dead; their poems are littered with phrases like "her maidenhood," or "twixt the sea and thy shore"—and such diction, used in earnest, ensures that no reader will take them seriously. Consider your word choices in terms of both their denotative, literal meaning, and their connotations—what they suggest and imply.

3. Point of view. You should try out every possible point of view, to expand your choices and learn how each functions. Many writers get stuck in the first person singular; they never get away from "I woke up. I looked around. I thought about my life." First-person poems need not be avoided; but many writers seem to think they're the only option available. And a common difficulty, when you're starting out, is that you feel you have to tell "the truth" if you're writing in first person. A poem is a work of imagination, not your autobiography. You shouldn't let your poem be stifled by "what really happened." Sometimes putting your poem into third person—"He woke up. He looked around. He thought about his life."—can help you get some needed perspective, shake you loose from actual events, and let you invent as the poem needs it. First-person plural—the "we" voice—can be an interesting choice, too; it enlarges the scope from the personal to the collective. Then there's "you," which might either be an address to a specific person—lots of love poems get addressed to a "you," creating a feeling of intimacy—or which might simply mean, "one." A "you" poem can also address the reader.

4. Syntax and grammar. Take a close look at how you tend to put your sentences together. Do you typically write short sentences, or long elaborate ones, or something in between? Do you load up the adjectives before your nouns? Maybe you have a bad habit like using passive voice, or overusing a word like "which" or "that." Ezra Pound said, "poetry should be at least as well-written as prose," and we agree; bad grammar doesn't fly for either one. You have to know what the rules are in order to break them in a way that serves your poem, so if you don't know the basics, get help and read the chapter, "A Grammatical Excursion." One common fault we've seen is inconsistency in things like using capitals and punctuation. Whether to use them or not is your choice, but a random scattering—capitals sometimes, proper punctuation sometimes, with mysterious lapses—will only distract your reader and make her think you don't really know what you're doing. If you feel enslaved by the sentence, try writing fragments, breaking apart words, playing with their arrangement on the page, as E. E. Cummings did and as many contemporary experimental writers are doing.

5. Form: line breaks, stanzas, structure. As with point of view, you
should try out all the various possible arrangements for your poems.
If you always write in one solid stanza, it's time to begin experimenting: couplets, tercets, quatrains. The same for line breaks—try some
different ways of doing them. If you always write free verse, try adding
some formal requirements—meter or rhyme or some other pattern
you must work with. If you always write in iambic pentameter, break
out into something less structured. Also take a look at whether your
poems as a whole follow a structural pattern—do they always end
with an image? With a "punch line"? Try ending with an abstract
statement, or something less conclusive, more open-ended. Maybe
they always circle back to something they began with; if so, make
yourself—let yourself—write something that keeps going outward.
Get away from starting your lines at the left margin, and use the field
of the page.

6. Imagery. We all have particular words and images that seem to
crop up in the course of our work. You may notice that you fill your
poems with images of mothers, or couples, or animals. A good thing
to look at is the *kinds* of images you make—are they vague and confusing, or sharp and detailed? Do you use too many similes—or not
enough? Do you rely on statements—"She made me feel so sexy"—
to the exclusion of images which might embody some of your
thoughts and ideas? Less common is the opposite problem: image
after image without any abstract statement. Usually, image and statement combine in a poem (though there are memorable exceptions).
Notice what your balance is, and see if you need to strengthen one or
the other.

7. Any other pattern that you perceive. Know your own work. Being
aware of your stylistic strengths and weaknesses will not only help you
to grow, but will help you to deal with criticism from others.
Everyone has certain things they can do well, and other areas that
need work. Maybe you have great details in your poems, but have
trouble making them add up to a coherent whole. If you know this,
you won't feel so defensive when someone says, "This doesn't hold
together." Instead, you'll recognize that again you've run up against

your limitations—and you'll be grateful for suggestions to help you overcome them. Maybe you're too literal and linear, and need to make some associative leaps; the next chapter on dreams and experiments can help lead you away from the logical. Read the symbolist and surrealist writers, and Spanish poet Federico Garciá Lorca's *Poet in New York*. Read and reread the work of Chilean poet Pablo Neruda, whose earthy, compassionate verse often contains surrealistic, magical images. Try contemporary writers like Mei-Mei Berssenbrugge, Ron Silliman, and Leslie Scalapino, who all have unique and intriguing ways of making poems—and read anyone who doesn't make logical sense to you. Write whatever comes into your head, without stopping; write down your dreams; let go. If you have the opposite problem and no one *ever* understands your poems, though you think you're communicating something perfectly clearly—if your work has been deemed obscure by several readers who are otherwise astute, intelligent, literate people—you may need to focus on clarity, on what you intend to say and what is being heard by others. Of course, we can't always see our own patterns, especially in the heat of new writing. That's not the time, anyway, for thinking about these things. But when you're ready to step back and demand the best from your poem, see if you can regard your work objectively—and invite other readers to help you do that.

There's another aspect of voice to consider: the persona poem. *Persona* is Greek for mask; in a persona poem, you pretend to be someone else. In truth, all poems are in a sense persona poems—the "I" of a first-person poem that seems to be about the poet's true experience is just as much of a construction as a poem in the voice of a medieval peasant speaking to us from the dead. In the latter case, though, we'd never mistake the peasant's voice for the poet's; a persona poem usually announces itself. Such poems are a great way to stretch your style. You may find you need to change it completely for the sake of the person you're creating on the page. And a persona poem can let you explore events and states of being more freely; masks allow us to shed our ordinary identities. Frank Bidart has written beautifully as various characters, including the famous Russian dancer Nijinsky and an anorexic young woman; when you read these and others of his poems, you'll recognize his particular style. Ai has also written a number of persona poems, one in the voices of John and Bobby Kennedy. Rita Dove's book about her grandparents, *Thomas and Beulah*, sometimes presents their experiences from the first person. Michael Ondaatje's *The Collected Works of Billy the Kid* brings alive the voices of a particular time and place.

This poem by Richard Jones not only portrays a woman of ancient China, but does it in the style of early Chinese poetry, at least as it sounds rendered in English. This would be a good time to acquaint yourself with poets like Wang Wei, Tu Fu, and Li Po. Read some translations by Sam Hamill, or Willis and Tony Barnstone, or earlier translations by Arthur Whaley. A good recent anthology is *A Drifting Boat: Chinese Zen Poetry* from White Pine Press.

WAN CHU'S WIFE IN BED

Wan Chu, my adoring husband,
has returned from another trip
selling trinkets in the provinces.
He pulls off his lavender shirt
as I lie naked in our bed,
waiting for him. He tells me
I am the only woman he'll ever love.
He may wander from one side of China
to the other, but his heart
will always stay with me.
His face glows in the lamplight
with the sincerity of a boy
when I lower the satin sheet
to let him see my breasts.
Outside, it begins to rain
on the cherry trees
he planted with our son,
and when he enters me with a sigh,
the storm begins in earnest,
shaking our little house.
Afterwards, I stroke his back

until he falls asleep.
I'd love to stay awake all night
listening to the rain,
but I should sleep, too.
Tomorrow Wan Chu will be
a hundred miles away
and I will be awake all night
in the arms of Wang Chen,
the tailor from Ming Pao,
the tiny village down river.

Jones's poem, with its surprising and amusing revelation of the wife's betrayal, makes these readers, at least, question Wan Chu's declarations of love as well. The voice convinces us with its quiet, straightforward style. The simplicity and clarity are characteristic not only of the translated Chinese poems we've read, but also of Jones's other work.

This next poem, by Patricia Smith, adopts a very different tone and style which suits its speaker — a white supremacist.

SKINHEAD

They call me skinhead, and I got my own beauty.
It is knife-scrawled across my back in sore, jagged letters,
it's in the way my eyes snap away from the obvious.
I sit in my dim matchbox,
on the edge of a bed tousled with my ragged smell,
slide razors across my hair,
count how many ways
I can bring blood closer to the surface of my skin.
These are the duties of the righteous,
the ways of the anointed.

The face that moves in my mirror is huge and pockmarked,
scraped pink and brilliant, apple-cheeked,
I am filled with my own spit.
Two years ago, a machine that slices leather
sucked in my hand and held it,
whacking off three fingers at the root.

I didn't feel nothing till I looked down
and saw one of them on the floor
next to my boot heel,
and I ain't worked since then.

I sit here and watch niggers take over my TV set,
walking like kings up and down the sidewalks in my head,
walking like their fat black mamas *named* them freedom.
My shoulders tell me that ain't right.
So I move out into the sun
where my beauty makes them lower their heads,
or into the night
with a lead pipe up my sleeve,
a razor tucked in my boot.
I was born to make things right.

It's easy now to move my big body into shadows,
to move from a place where there was nothing
into the stark circle of a streetlight,
the pipe raised up high over my head.
It's a kick to watch their eyes get big,
round and gleaming like cartoon jungle boys,
right in that second when they know
the pipe's gonna come down, and I got this thing
I like to say, listen to this, I like to say
"Hey, nigger, Abe Lincoln's been dead a long time."

I get hard listening to their skin burst.
I was born to make things right.

Then this newspaper guy comes around,
seems I was a little sloppy kicking some fag's ass
and he opened his hole and screamed about it.
This reporter finds me curled up in my bed,
those TV flashes licking my face clean.
Same ol' shit.
Ain't got no job, the coloreds and spics got 'em all.
Why ain't I working? Look at my hand, asshole.
No, I ain't part of no organized group,
I'm just a white boy who loves his race,
fighting for a pure country.

Sometimes it's just me. Sometimes three. Sometimes 30.
AIDS will take care of the faggots,
then it's gon' be white on black in the streets.
Then there'll be three million.
I tell him that.

So he writes it up
and I come off looking like some kind of freak,
like I'm Hitler himself. I ain't that lucky,
but I got my own beauty.
It is in my steel-toed boots,
in the hard corners of my shaved head.

I look in the mirror and hold up my mangled hand,
only the baby finger left, sticking straight up,
I know it's the wrong goddamned finger,
but fuck you all anyway.
I'm riding the top rung of the perfect race,
my face scraped pink and brilliant.
I'm your baby, America, your boy,
drunk on my own spit, I am goddamned fuckin' beautiful.

And I was born

and raised

right here.

In this piece, Smith, a black woman poet, sounds like a white male racist. This boy comes alive on the page; we can hear and feel his hate and anger. (Smith, who was a National Poetry Slam winner, brings it out even more powerfully in performance.) Interestingly, we're also drawn to, or at least compelled by, this boy who is both physically and psychically damaged. He has a sense of himself as beautiful, as purposeful: "I was born to make things right." His violence makes sense to him, and this is what the poem illuminates: the world-view of a radically different other. Smith gets at the issues here by moving out of her own perspective. It wasn't enough to ask the question, "What makes a person like this tick, what makes him do these things?" Smith goes deeper to find her answers, and they are uncomfortable ones, not meant to reassure us but to make us look more carefully and thoughtfully.

Persona poems are shapeshifting, a chance to move beyond the boundaries of our personality, our particular circumstances. If we enter our imagination fully and deeply enough, we can experience our questions, our concerns and obsessions, with more empathy and insight. And whatever voices speak from that deep place will require attention.

IDEAS FOR WRITING

1. Do a stylistic analysis of a poet you like. You might want to start by using our checklist in this chapter, examining subject matter, diction, imagery, and the like; try to discover what sorts of moves the writer characteristically makes. Then write a poem in that writer's style.

2. Now do a *parody* of the same poet. A parody takes aspects of a writer's style and exaggerates them for comic effect.

3. Here's a tough one: swallow your pride and do a parody of your *own* style. This can be a lot of fun—trust us.

4. Try to write a poem that is the opposite of your style in every way.

5. Take a poem you've written and "translate" it into:

   academic-intellectual diction

   romantic diction

   colloquial speech (this might be black dialect, or southern dialect, or East Coast dialect, or any other way of speaking that isn't mainstream, conventional English)

6. Write a poem in first-person singular about something that happened to somebody else; tell it as though it happened to you.

7. Take something that happened to you, and tell it in third person.

8. Write a poem that knows it's a poem and that addresses the reader; step out from behind the poem and talk about the act of writing or what the poem is doing (or trying to). Some poems you could read first are "Portrait" by Pattiann Rogers; "The Truth" by Dick Bakken; "Leaves That Grow Inward" by Susan Mitchell.

9. Write a poem in the voice of someone in your family. It might be one of your parents talking about their lives or how they met; a brother or sister describing some family gathering. If you want, you can include yourself as a person in the poem—seen, of course, from the speaker's perspective.

10. Write a poem in the voice of a famous person, living or dead. Try to give the reader an intimate glimpse of this person, one that couldn't be gotten from the media or history books.

11. What kind of character seems most foreign to you—a homeless man? A suburban housewife? A Zen monk? Whoever it is, that's the persona to adopt. Find a way to enter that character's experience, and write a poem in his or her voice.

12. Research a period of history that interests you, and write a poem that purports to be excerpts from the journal of someone who lived during that time.

Stop Making Sense:
Dreams and Experiments

after the election

our teeth rattle & our souls.
from the socket of the mask
mice swarm & swans.
the mother's eye is running.
a small boy spins thru
the furnace of grass,
thru wheat spear & spire
goes running.
deep in the soil deep in the gut
death's bird-blue calyx is humming

—Michael Koch

Earlier in this book, we said that there's something in a good poem that can't be accounted for logically. If poems were only logical constructions, anyone could study the rules, glue a few phrases together, and assemble a fine piece of work—just like putting together a model airplane or painting a portrait by numbers. Ironically, what would be missing would be the very thing that was essential: the poetry itself. When we say of some gesture or experience, "That was pure poetry," we aren't talking about meter, or similes, or line breaks; we mean that something ineffable, something beautiful and even beyond words, has touched us. When a poem moves us, it's not simply that the writer has dazzled us with technique, but that some sort of emotional energy has leaped from the words on the page, energy that we then experience. Emily Dickinson said she knew a good poem when, after reading it, she felt as though the top of her head were coming off.

Mystery, creativity, inspiration—these are the words that come to mind when we think about certain aspects of poetry that are separate from craft. These are things that can't neccessarily be taught, or learned. What we can do is to try and access that source from which they spring, to circumvent or suspend the logical, literal, linear mind with its need to control and understand everything.

The *surrealists* were a group of French writers and artists who, beginning in the 1920s, took a stand against logic and rational thought by turning to dreams and the subconscious mind as sources for their work. Their poems are characterized by fantastic images, wild leaps of imagination, and a resistance to logical interpretation. Their aim was liberation—not merely of poetry from the conventions that bound it, but of the spirit. And as the poet André Bréton pointed out at the time, such ideas were not new. The surrealists had the example of an earlier group of French poets, the *symbolists*, who wanted to create symbols of a reality beyond sense, and then writers like Arthur Rimbaud who saw the poet as an ecstatic seer and advocated "derangement of the senses" in order to transcend ordinary states of consciousness. Centuries before the surrealists or their immediate predecessors, people of all cultures placed a high importance on dreams and visions as a means to spiritual knowledge. Throughout the ages, people have enacted rituals that involve ingesting hallucinogenic plants, fasting, sweating, self-flagellation, and other practices with the aim of contacting levels of awareness unavailable to the everyday self. Even today, with the apparent triumph of rationalism and materialism in many places, the mysterious, nonrational impulse continually breaks through. In some cultures it survives relatively intact, though it's doubtful that this will be the case too much longer, considering the encroachments of so-called "civilized" societies. But the need to experience nonordinary reality is everywhere evident, from children who spin in circles to watch the world tilt, to the use of alcohol or drugs or loud music, to the complete silence of a meditation retreat.

How does this translate into poetic practice? A poetry that seeks to subvert logical connections has as its operative principles surprise, juxtaposition, openness, and movement rather than predictability, linearity, closure, and stasis. It might focus on highlighting gaps and fragments, rather than on avoiding them. It might let the language lead the writer into whatever meaning was to be found, rather than the writer beginning with something she meant to say and then trying to find the words to articulate what she already knows. These are, in fact, all ways of writing that have been increasingly used by writers in the twentieth century, though a number of them have seen it as a linguistic rather than a spiritual enterprise. For many writers, the focus has shifted from language as a means to an end—whether that end is communication, self-knowledge, or spiritual awareness—to focusing on the language itself, occasionally *as* the end. Poems about language, or poems that attempt to enact themselves in language as they happen—these stem from different ideas about poetry than, say, a personal poem or a poem of witness which seeks to use language in its conventional sense to portray an event. Another way to think about it, since we're trying to simplify some pretty complex ideas, is this: modern and postmodern poetry have more and more made language itself the subject of the poem and center of attention, rather than using language as a more or less "invisible" tool.

Before we explore these ideas further, let's look at a contemporary poem by Jan Richman that falls somewhere between conventional uses of language and complete subversion. Richman's poem is thoroughly modern in a number of ways: in its irony, its conscious play with language, and its juxtapositions. The poem invades the familiar story of Dr. Jekyll and Mr. Hyde to transform it for the writer's purposes, and is comfortable along the way including a line from "Little Red Riding Hood," a Dream Date lunchbox, and a reference to Sylvia Plath's poem "Daddy" (Plath refers to the father in her poem as "Herr Doctor, Herr Enemy").

YOU'VE CHANGED, DR. JEKYLL

My, what big teeth you have. And I can't help but notice
your inseam sneak up to your chin and beard your uncircum-
stance. Your lace collar shudders, and . . . Now you remember:
Smile, an ordinary word. Chat. Beat. Brag. While your left hand
conducts an under-the-table ejaculation, your right
flips the rusty tongue of a Dream Date lunchbox, airing
its contents: laboratory mythologies. Yawn. Why do
historical men either gorge or starve? Come midnight,
you'll paint the town red, your lips wrapped around
a block-long siren, greased and bawling like a burned baby.
Now you're in the parlor deciphering forgeries.
Good eye. But what's that stain? You're due at the Nobels'
for dinner in an hour. Herr Doctor, Mr. Dad, you've handed
down a scratchy decree, this cushion on which I sit to jerk
off in the meager poem of your hiding place. Five hot minutes
on the phone with legacy equals a cup of serum. Hallelujah!
Accepting the award for Mlle. Hyde is cultured silence
braying like a Baptist: Oh yes, I can love all things,
just not at the same time.

Some of this poem seems surreal, dream-like: Dr. Jekyll's "lips
wrapped around / a block-long siren" is an eerie image, and the lips
seem to then be transformed into that "bawling" baby, who is
"burned." Dr. Jekyll seems to be slipping out of his good-guy persona,
like the wolf in "Little Red Riding Hood" whose canines are apparent,
even when he's dressed up like the grandmother he's devoured in the
fable. And he seems faintly ridiculous, too, with his inseam "sneaking
up" and his Dream Date lunchbox. The narrator mocks this character as "Herr Doctor, Mr. Dad," but beneath that is a personal revelation: the narrator's father apparently has a dark side and is a Mr. Hyde
figure. Is "Mlle. Hyde," then, the narrator's mother, who is absent—
someone is accepting an award for her—and whose presence is
replaced by "cultured silence"? The poem doesn't reveal its meanings
easily, or completely; it leaves gaps, deals with its subject matter
obliquely, requires that the reader recognize some of its strategies.

Many poets currently writing have gone far beyond recording their dreams, or writing whatever occurs to them for fifteen minutes, or yoking unlikely things together simply for the sake of the new. These are all worthwhile writing exercises—dreams, especially, are sometimes so richly associative and intriguing that transcribing them faithfully can lead you to fascinating material. But let's try to delve a little further into notions of nonlinearity, into why it might be fruitful to explore more options for your poetry than straightforward description or narration.

One useful thing to remember is that words—however sensuously they may evoke the world—are not the world. You may beautifully describe a flower opening, but the flower you create in words is a virtual flower; it can't be picked, or left to bloom by the roadside. From this obvious starting point, it follows that we can't ever capture the world "out there" and set it down on the page. There's always a gap between the word and the thing. We can't ever, in language, recreate the totality of our experience—which may involve what we encounter through our senses, a complex of emotional responses, and what we think and remember and desire, all at the same time. We can't know how something actually feels for another person; we can't crawl inside their skin. Language itself becomes an analogy— what something is *like* rather than what something *is*.

Poetry is always, inevitably an experience *in language*—and not necessarily the experience you want to convey, since each person who reads the poem will bring to it his or her own ideas, beliefs, prejudices, intellect, emotions, awareness, cultural background, and individual experiences. The question of communication, then, becomes a slippery one. Just what is being said in your poem depends partly on who is hearing it. This is why taste is so individual, why one person loves a poem that leaves someone else cold. In a very real sense, each one is reading a different poem.

Of course, a writer can narrow down ranges of possible interpretations; sheer chaos is generally not the aim of poets. When a poem begins with the words "the fighter pilot" instead of "he," the specificity keeps us from wondering who "he" is and beginning to make up our own answer, and so getting distracted from what the writer would like us to focus on. If you want to write a poignant poem about a child dying in the streets of Sarajevo, it probably won't serve your purpose if your language is so imprecise that everyone thinks you're talking about your inner child. We think the key here is *intent*; do you want to narrow the possibilities for the reader, and does this narrowing serve your purpose or defeat it? Do you want to widen the possibilities and allow for more ambiguity, more multiplicity of meaning? Is it important to you to communicate something, and if so, what? Is it your intent to challenge your reader and the conventional meanings of words? Why or why not? What's the difference between mystery and obscurity, and how valuable to you is each? Who is your audience? Does audience matter? Is language about describing experience, or can language and experience be separated at all? Is nonlinear language, with its ellipses, its disjunctions, a more accurate rendering of how we perceive the world than narrative is? These are important questions for a writer to consider. They need to be explored fully and honestly before you can develop your own poetics, your sense of what you are trying to do with language, and why.

There's one more crucial element we haven't mentioned—a sense of play. When you fool around with language, freed from the constraints of conventional syntax, grammar, meaning, you can more easily access that part of the brain where creative consciousness resides. In the visual arts, there's a trick for drawing that involves turning a picture of an object upside down before trying to copy it. The novice artist no longer tries to render a chair, or a bowl of fruit, but lines and curves and shadows. Anything that changes the way you habitually see or do something will tend to open new perspectives, new possibilities. Familiarity breeds not contempt so much as blindness; as we grow more habitual we lose the freshness of our perceptions, which is what children have in such abundance. So whether you feel resistant to letting go your grip on logic, or ecstatic at the thought of breaking out from the confines of conventional language, we urge you to try the exercises in this chapter in the spirit of creative play, to let your dream-self explore without judgment, to trust that raw chaotic place where the poems begin.

IDEAS FOR WRITING

1. We said that recording dreams can be a worthwhile exercise. Try keeping a notebook or tape recorder by your bed for a week, and jotting down dreams, or saying them, as soon as you wake, when they're still vivid. Don't try to do anything more than record them, in as much detail as you remember. After you finish the notations, go back and reread, or listen. Work with whatever now strikes you as fresh and interesting, and combine the best lines into one poem.

2. Many people have recurring dreams—of flying, of being chased, of being in a particular location or situation. Write a poem about such a dream that uses repetition to capture its obsessive nature. Try to repeat fragments rather than simply initial words or complete sentences; let the repetition interrupt the flow of the dream-story.

3. Do some research on dream interpretation, Freudian or otherwise, and write a poem in which two voices speak: the dreamer and the analyzer. You might have them alternate lines, or interrupt each other; you could separate them by using different typography, or mix them together so it's hard to know who's speaking when.

4. "Exquisite Corpse" is a game invented by the surrealists that can be done by a group. Each person writes a line, then passes the poem to the next person with the previous lines hidden (the page can be folded over to cover each new line). Try this with people writing anything they want, and try it again with everyone doing something similar—beginning with the same word, or including a natural object, or anything else you think of that will allow for a sense of both predictability and chance.

5. Write a poem that steals from other, well-known texts, altering them in some small way so that the originals are recognizable. You might, for example, alter the famous opening of Charles

Dickens's novel *Great Expectations* by saying, "It was the best of times, it was the first of times." Let this alteration trigger a poem, or play with the poem by including several such lines.

6. Write a number of sentences that seem to follow the conventions of a story, but don't tell a story. Use words like "once," "suddenly," "then," "finally," and whatever else you notice about how stories unfold; but make the "plot" nonsensical.

7. Leaf through several books of poetry at random and jot down a list of words that strike you. Don't pore over the poems; this works best if you don't pay any attention to the context, but simply write down words that appeal to you. Choose twenty of these and write a poem which uses them, adding as few new words as possible.

8. If you keep a journal of your daily activities, thoughts, emotions, go back to entries that are at least a year old. Again, don't read for context; simply write down whatever jumps out at you from the page—a word, a phrase, a sentence. Ideally, after skimming a number of pages, you'll have material that has personal and emotional resonance but is no longer tied to a particular situation or story. Such fragments can be compelling and powerful without falling into predictable patterns.

9. A *collage* poem is simple: find several sources of language and put them together. This usually works best if you have some different kinds of language—say, a love letter, a book of postmodern literary theory, an issue of *Hustler*. You can go through, circling interesting words and phrases to transcribe, or get out the scissors and begin cutting and rearranging. This can be a good tool for revising one of your old, failed poems; cut it up and throw it into the mix, and see what emerges.

10. Using a poem you've already written, invent some arbitrary principle for arranging words on the field of the page and rearrange your own poem accordingly. Lyn Hejinian wrote a piece in which words beginning with "a" were placed at the left margin,

words beginning with "b" started one space in, and so on. You might put nouns in one place, verbs in another, prepositions in a third position; or words that relate to emotion at the bottom, words that relate to intellect at the top; or any other interesting organizational pattern you can think of. See what this does to your language, and whether, and how, it changes the meanings.

11. Write an exhaustively detailed account, in prose, of something that happened to you. Then go back and try cutting out various things to see what happens. Cut out every other sentence, or every fourth word, or every second noun. Play with the results, and put them into lines.

12. Jot down scraps of conversation that you hear over a one-week period—at the office, on the bus, on the radio, in the park, wherever. Take these scraps and weave them together into a poem that seems to follow the usual conventions of language— that is, let each part seamlessly connect to the other. Here's a brief example:

> He wanted to tell her about it
> but the horse was old and going blind
> from one end of town to the other

Meter, Rhyme, and Form

In contemporary poetry, free verse is the norm. Pick up an anthology such as *New American Poets of the '90's* (published by David Godine) or *Up Late* (Four Walls Eight Windows), or the annual *Best American Poetry*—or any of the many poetry collections over the past few decades. You're likely to find few sonnets or villanelles or rondeaus—all traditional forms that were commonly used by poets in previous times. Instead, you'll see lines of varying lengths, flowing down the page without a predetermined rhythm; you'll hear sounds echoing from word to word, through rhyme and other techniques, but there won't be any particular pattern to where and when those sounds occur.

Until recent times, most poetry written in English used meter, and often a rhyme scheme as well. Walt Whitman's *Leaves of Grass*, which was first published—in fact, self-published—in 1855, was the ground swell for the wave of free verse that would soon sweep over American poetry. In the beginning of the twentieth century, poets who broke away from traditional forms were rebelling against what they experienced as the tyranny of certain formal requirements. Ezra Pound, in his preface to a 1916 anthology titled *Some Imagist Poets*, helped define a poetics that had a tremendous influence on the way poetry came to be thought about and written; besides the emphasis on concrete, specific imagery as an important technique, Pound and other so-called imagists broke free of the restraints of meter. They wanted, as Pound wrote:

To create a new rhythm—as the expression of new moods—and not to copy old rhythms, which merely echo old moods. We do not insist upon "free-verse" as the only method of writing poetry. We fight for it as a principle of liberty. We believe that the individuality of a poet may often be better expressed in free-verse than in conventional form. In poetry, a new cadence means a new idea.

The poets since then have overwhelmingly agreed; today, only a few poets write in traditional forms more than occasionally, and many developing writers have never learned the structure of a sonnet, much less attempted one themselves. Lately, though, there's been increasing interest in a return to, or at least a reexamination of, traditional formal elements like meter and end-rhymes. Some people have suggested that maybe the baby was thrown out along with the bathwater, and that there may be good reason to take another look at the techniques which produced so many magnificent poems in previous centuries. The issue, of course, isn't whether anyone *should* write free verse or formal; that decision should come out of the poem's requirements, out of the integration of form and content. Free verse, after all, has form, too. And it could also be said that each individual poem, whether in free verse or a traditional form, has its own unique, specific form. But we think it's significant that the imagists and other poets were familiar with the formal tradition *before* they made the then-radical shift to free verse. They knew all about the effects that could be achieved with various meters, and that discipline was a good basis for formulating free verse lines that were rhythmically alive and interesting. These writers had extensive ear-training; they knew how to *hear* the music of language, and skillfully used that knowledge when they turned to free verse.

That music was apparent, too, to listeners in the days when poetry was an oral tradition, the myths and stories of the culture passed on in the speaking or singing voice. Today, many of us tend to read primarily with our eyes and our minds—studying the words, trying to make meaning, to pick up the writer's nuances of thought and imagery. We don't often enough read poems aloud, to let the lan-

guage vibrate through our rib cage and vocal chords, to savor the deli-
cious taste of syllables on our tongue. And so we deprive ourselves of
one of the crucial pleasures of poetry. As children, we all loved saying nursery rhymes aloud, or repeating tongue twisters like "She sells
sea shells by the sea shore." We delighted in language not only for its
necessary function of helping us communicate, but for the sheer
physical satisfaction of saying things. That delight is one of the fundamental bases of poetry; so if you find your attention to listening is
rather rusty, start developing it by reading poems aloud—your own
and others—and attending live poetry readings. Pick up some cas-
settes of poets reading their work, or the work of other poets. Being
stuck in traffic takes on a whole new meaning when Galway Kinnell
is on your tape deck, soothing and inspiring you with those rolling,
expansive lines from Whitman.

What has all this to do with meter and rhyme? Plenty. Because
meter and rhyme are ultimately about the *sounds* of language. Meter
is organized rhythm; rhyme has to do with echo, with a hearing again
of a note that's been played before. Such formal elements are at the
roots of poetry in English, just as classical music is a source for contemporary composers, or the blues was a jumping-off point for rock
'n roll.

So we think it's important not only to be familiar with traditional
forms—after all, you'd want to recognize a sonnet or a villanelle
when it popped up in your reading—but to experiment with writing
them as well. And trying on such forms needn't be like putting on a
straitjacket. In fact, if you've never had to make creative use of language to fit a formal requirement, you're in for a pleasant surprise.
Yes, it's challenging and often difficult, but it may well send you
down interesting paths you wouldn't have taken otherwise. The
restrictions of form push you to be more resourceful, to find the language you need. This not only teaches you a lot about language, but
it's also a lot of fun. Then, too, a number of writers have found that
difficult emotional material may be more easily handled within some
sort of defined boundaries; the restraints of meter, a rhyme scheme,
or some pattern of repetition may help put the brakes on runaway
material. But don't take their, or our, word for it. Try some of the

exercises following this chapter and see for yourself. First, though, you'll need to know a bit about the common meters in English, and about rhyme.

Meter

Meter comes from the Greek for "measure." Every poem has rhythm, but when the rhythm is highly organized into a pattern where the number of syllables is important, as well as whether those syllables are stressed or not then we have meter. (Remember from "The Music of the Line" that a *stressed* syllable gets a little push, an unstressed or *slack* syllable doesn't. The word "sparrow" consists of a stressed syllable followed by a slack: SPARrow.)

The unit of measure that we pay attention to when talking about meter is called a *foot*. Here are the names of the most common feet in English (a ʊ marks a slack syllable; a (/) marks a stressed one):

iamb (ʊ /): create, inspire, tonight, motel
trochee (/ ʊ): hungry, snowfall, argue, orchid
dactyl (/ ʊ ʊ): longitude, messages, miracle, video
anapest (ʊ ʊ /): by the edge, intertwine, in the end
spondee (/ /): trap door, new shoes, blind pig

The other part of meter is knowing how many of these feet occur in each line. For example, read the following sentence aloud:

In metric verse the meter keeps the beat.

In terms of stresses and slack syllables, you should hear: daDUM daDUM daDUM daDUM daDUM. That's a pretty easy pattern to pick out: five daDUMS, five iambs. You've just identified the most commonly used meter: iambic pentameter. *Penta*, of course, is a prefix from the Latin, for five. All the meters are described in this way; if the above sentence had read, "In metric verse the meter counts," you would have had four iambs, or iambic tetrameter. So depending on how many feet are in each line, you can then label them:

monometer—one foot per line
dimeter—two feet
trimeter—three feet
tetrameter—four feet

pentameter—five feet
hexameter—six feet
and so forth

Scansion is the term used to talk about reading poetry in this way, paying attention to the prevailing meter. Scansion is not always, however, a precise technique. How do you pronounce the word "details"? Some people say DEtails, pronouncing it as a trochee. Many newscasters choose the iamb: "Rock star pleads not guilty, deTAILS at six." One of your authors says TEEvee for the television; the other hears it as a spondee: TEEVEE. Such regionalisms may affect your reading of a line; and some stressed syllables may sound, to your ear, more stressed than others, though there's no system of notation for this. And, finally, here's the real trick to meter: it's more appropriately considered as the pattern *behind* the sounds you actually hear.

Confused? It is really not as complicated as it seems. Think of how boring it would be to always clump along going daDUM daDUM daDUM daDUM daDUM in everything you wrote. You'd sound, pretty quickly, like a nursery rhymer and not a poet. Many nursery rhymes, in fact, *are* written in that strict a meter. That's why they're so easy to remember: strict meter, strict rhyme. But poets try for more subtle effects. You're not out to hit your reader over the head. When meter is working well, it announces its presence clearly but quietly. It hums along steadily behind the actual sounds of the words, keeping the beat without intruding.

The best way to understand this is first to read and hear poems written in meter, and then to practice writing some yourself. Read Shakespeare's plays and sonnets to get a feel for iambic pentameter— or just about any other poet writing in English since Chaucer's time. Then get hold of some contemporary examples (there are some suggestions for reading at the end of this chapter), so you don't think that you need to include a lot of "thee"s and "thou"s and "fie on't"s in your own efforts. You don't want to sound old-fashioned just because you're using something from the past. Language has changed since Shakespeare, and writing in the living language means your poems will be alive, too, not mummified in dead syntax and usages.

Let's look for a minute at how Shakespeare used iambic pentameter, so you get a feel for what we mean when we say that meter is the pattern behind the actual sounds of the words. This example is from *Hamlet*:

> O, that this too too sullied flesh would melt,
> Thaw and resolve itself into a dew!
> Or that the Everlasting had not fix'd
> His canon 'gainst self-slaughter! O God! God!
> How weary, stale, flat and unprofitable,
> Seem to me all the uses of this world!

Read this cheerful passage over a couple of times. It's in iambic pentameter, but there isn't a line that clunks along in strict daDUMs. Yet listen carefully, and you'll definitely hear it. Sometimes there's an extra syllable or two; sometimes he begins, not with the unstressed syllable, but with a stressed one: "O" and "Thaw." Such rhythms are more complex and interesting than any strict adherence to the pattern. But they depend on our hearing a pattern, so that they can play with that, can follow it or work against it. If you're familiar with how jazz improvisation works, that's a useful analogy: after the melody gets established, the soloist takes off in a new direction while the same chord changes are repeated. The meter establishes your pattern; then you, the soloist, get to dazzle your audience with variations and departures.

Meter can have an exciting effect on your language. Without it, it's you and the blank page; with it, you have some tension, something to pull you and to push back against. Meter can help you establish a certain distance between you and your reader, which could be useful if you're dealing with highly intense material. It can be a way of ordering chaotic emotions and experiences, which, come to think of it, is one thing poetry does anyway. Meter is a little added artifice, a heightening of the awareness that this thing you're making is not just a journal entry or a record of your thoughts. It's a way to work with those thoughts in a manner that constantly reminds you that language and rhythm—the *way* in which you say something—are as crucial as *what* you are saying.

Rhyme

Everyone knows what rhyme is. That's the thing that poems are supposed to do, right? Only now poems don't rhyme, do they? In fact, poems *do* still rhyme—even those written in free verse. Rhyme is based on similar sounds, and English is full of words that echo each other. It's true that free verse poets don't usually use *end rhyme*, the practice of placing rhyming words at the ends of lines—at least, not on a regular basis. They're more likely to use *internal rhyme*— to rhyme a word *within* a line with another word in that line, or with one in the next line; or maybe a word within a line with the word at the end of that line. But a regular pattern of rhymes at the end of each line is a characteristic of formal verse, not free. Here's an example of end rhyme, an excerpt from a Robert Frost poem:

> The shattered water made a misty din,
> Great waves looked over others coming in,
> And thought of doing something to the shore
> That water never did to land before.

By the way, did you pick up the meter in Frost's poem? When we said iambic pentameter was common, we weren't kidding. You'll also notice there is a *rhyme scheme*, a pattern to the end rhymes. Letters are commonly used to show such patterns, the letter changing each time the rhyme changes. In the case of this example, the rhyme scheme so far is *aabb*.

Look over these three lines from a contemporary poet, Ai, and notice her use of internal rhyme:

> I'm not afraid of the blade
> you've just pointed at my head.
> If I were dead, you could take the boy . . .

Two rhymes stand out immediately: "afraid" and "blade" in the first line, and "head" and "dead" in the second and third. Such rhymes are called *strict*, or *pure*, or *perfect* rhymes. The initial sound of the word is different, but the rest is identical. Moon–June, trace–face, believe–relieve, go for it–show for it. Many people think that this is the only kind of rhyme, but luckily for poets, it isn't. Look again at Ai's lines, at the words "blade" and "head." They aren't strict rhyme, but they do share a similarity of sounds; the vowels are different, but the ending consonants are alike. Such rhymes of words whose sounds are closely related, but not identical, are called *slant rhymes* (also known as *half rhymes* or *off rhymes*). Some examples of slant rhymes are face–dress, fear–care, blend–stand, here–chair.

There are other kinds of rhyme as well. *Apocopated*, or cut-off rhyme, occurs when the last syllable of one of the rhymes is missing: wet–netted, trap–happen, ease–treason. There's even something called *eye rhyme*, which doesn't have to do with sounds at all but is visual: plough–cough, inflate–considerate, happy–sky. And you can use the same word twice and get away with it—that's *identical rhyme*. Or you might use *vowel rhyme*, commonly known as *assonance*: slope–road, sway–great, slim–glitter.

Knowing you have all these options puts a whole new spin on the prospect of using rhyme in your poems. Rhyme, like meter, is a technique that works best when it doesn't call attention to itself. You want someone to be reading your poem, not following your rhyme scheme. If you're working with a pattern of end rhymes, try not to make them all strict—take advantage of slant rhyme and other possibilities. In free verse, you can still use internal rhyme and occasional end rhyme to unify the music of your poem.

Remember, too, that rhyme is related to meaning. A rhymed word stands out—you can use rhyme to emphasize important words. And because a rhyme is essentially an echo, it has a feeling of closure. We call out—we get an answer. There's something satisfying in that transaction, and free verse writers often take advantage of it to end their poems. Look at the last word of a number of free verse poems; then look back over the two or three lines before it. You'll find that sometimes there's a word that sets up that final word, a call and the answering echo.

A Traditional Form: The Sonnet

You know those ads that say, "If you see only one movie this year, see this one"? We want to say the same thing about the sonnet. If you experiment with writing in only one traditional form, this should be it. The sonnet has been enormously popular with poets, and you're not going to get very far in poetry before you encounter one. You've no doubt encountered one already: something from Shakespeare or Wordsworth or Elizabeth Barrett Browning or Edna St. Vincent Millay. If this sounds like intimidating company, don't worry. After all, those writers are dead. You're alive and writing, and you don't have to compete.

The sonnet originated in Italy; its name comes from the Italian *sonnetto*, meaning "little song." A sonnet is short—just fourteen lines. It's written in iambic pentameter, and it has a rhyme scheme. Actually there are three different rhyme schemes for the three different kinds of sonnets: *Italian* or *Petrarchan* (named after the poet Petrarch, who wrote many sonnets to his love, Laura); *English* or *Shakespearean* (named after guess who); and *Spenserian*, after the poet Edmund Spenser. The easiest one to write—or at least, the one in which you have to find the least rhymes—is the Shakespearean. Here are the rhyme schemes for each type of sonnet:

Petrarchan: The fourteen lines are divided into an *octet* (eight-line stanza) and *sestet* (six-line stanza) rhymed a–b–b–a–a–b–b–a and c–d–e–c–d–e (the sestet is sometimes varied).

Shakespearean: a–b–a–b–c–d–c–d–e–f–e–f–g–g.

Spenserian: The least commonly seen, this is a mix of the other two: a–b–a–b–b–c–b–c–c–d–c–d–e–e.

The original sonnet—the Italian one—took advantage of the great number of rhymes in that language. When English poets got hold of it, they devised a rhyme scheme that would be easier to handle in a language with fewer rhymes. Shakespearean and Petrarchan sonnets suggest different ways of developing your material, because of how the rhymes work. In the Petrarchan, an idea is commonly laid out in the octet. Then there's often a "turn" (*volta* in Italian), a shift of some sort; the sestet develops this new line of thought. That is, the shift in rhyming lends itself to a shift in the content of the poem—form and content working together. In the Shakespearean sonnet, there is also often a shift after the octet; but then, too, that final couplet pushes the poem towards some sort of two-line closing statement, since those two rhymes back to back at the end give a reader a strong sense of finality. The Spenserian sonnet, too, can end with a strong sense of closure — if you can get to the last two lines before losing your sanity.

Here's a contemporary Shakespearean sonnet by Molly Peacock:

THE LULL

The possum lay on the tracks fully dead.
I'm the kind of person who stops to look.
It was big and white with flies on its head,
a thick healthy hairless tail, and strong, hooked
nails on its racoon-like feet. It was a full
grown possum. It was sturdy and adult.
Only its head was smashed. In the lull
that it took to look, you took the time to insult
the corpse, the flies, the world, the fact that we were
traipsing in our dress shoes down the railroad tracks.
"That's disgusting." You said that. Dreams, brains, fur
and guts: what we are. That's my bargain, the Pax
Peacock, with the world. Look hard, life's soft. Life's cache
is flesh, flesh, and flesh.

The tone here is casual, conversational: "I'm the kind of person who stops to look." The friends are "traipsing" in their dress shoes; the narrator's friend exclaims, "That's disgusting." There's none of the elevated language we might be tempted to think a sonnet requires; the poem, in fact, takes us down to the gritty level of "the corpse, the flies, the world," insisting that we "look hard." Some lines stick pretty closely to iambic pentameter; some stretch the line out and out — we counted eight beats in that second-to-last line. And what about the end — how does she get away with three stresses, instead of five? Imagine if she'd written "Life's cache / is flesh, and flesh, and flesh, and flesh, and flesh." That would fit the meter, but the deliberate breaking of the pattern is more interesting. The line is cut off; we're stopped short by its abruptness. Perhaps it recalls the possum's life that has prematurely ended; but in any case, it calls attention to itself, and to the word "flesh." Saying it five times would have been too many. Remember, as a kid, how you could repeat a word like "dog" until it sounded completely meaningless? Then, too, there are three characters in this poem; maybe flesh is repeated once for each of them. The poet asks us not to turn away in disgust at the realization that for all of us, it all comes down to flesh.

Though she sometimes loosens the meter, Peacock's rhymes here are pretty strict. Notice, though, that she uses a lot of enjambment to keep those strict end rhymes from sounding too obvious; we get to the end of the line and move right on to see where she's going.

One tendency of contemporary writers has been to play with the sonnet form, to stretch it and expand it beyond the rules. Some writers develop their own quirky rhyme schemes, while sticking to the other requirements of the form. We've seen sixteen-line sonnets that faithfully follow the Shakespearean pattern, then add on an extra couplet at the end. And there are some pieces titled "Sonnet" that we can't, for the life of us, figure out why the writer thought there was any relationship—beyond, maybe, the original meaning of "little song"; they tend to be short, at least. The sonnet seems to have adapted well to the needs of all kinds of writers.

If you're curious about other traditional forms, we'd like to recommend two anthologies, both of which are listed in Appendix B at the end of the book. *Strong Measures* contains many contemporary examples of ballads, rondeaus, rhyme royal, and a wealth of other possibilities. There's also a handy index that gives a description of the requirements of each form and refers you to which poems are in that particular form. *A Formal Feeling Comes: Poems in Form by Contemporary Women* not only includes formal poems but brief essays by each writer. In the meantime, if you can't wait for the bookstore to open, the next two chapters will give you more food for thought.

IDEAS FOR WRITING

1. Try a few lines of *accentual* verse. That means you only count accents (stresses), without worrying about iambs and anapests.

Write four lines, making sure there are four stresses in each line. (You can have as many unstressed syllables as you need.) When you're comfortable with that, write four lines of three stresses each. Then write four lines in which you alternate the number of stresses: 4–3–4–3.

2. Write a poem in *blank verse*—unrhymed iambic pentameter. To get the rhythm going in your subconscious, first read a lot of blank verse: besides Shakespeare's plays, try Milton's *Paradise Lost*, or more recent works by Robert Frost—"Mending Wall," "Home Burial," and many others; or Wallace Stevens's "Sunday Morning." *Don't write anything* until you've spent at least half an hour reading.

3. Write four lines and use as much internal rhyme in them as possible. Push it to the point of ridiculousness. Don't try to write anything serious; just see how far you can go.

4. Write a "silly sonnet" using strict meter and rhyme—the obvious kind you're not supposed to write. These can be a lot of fun with a group of people, each person adding a line.

5. Write a serious sonnet following any of the three rhyme schemes, but forget about the meter; make the lines any length and rhythm that you want.

6. Write a free verse poem with a rhyme scheme you've invented. One we've tried is six-line stanzas rhyming a–b–c–c–b–a.

7. Take some raw material for a poem—notes, jotted images, thoughts—or use a failed poem from the bottom of the pile. Cast it into three different forms:

    iambic tetrameter (rhymed or unrhymed)

    rhymed couplets

    a limerick (you remember limericks, don't you?)

8. *Syllabic verse* counts only syllables, not accents. Marianne Moore was fond of syllabics. Look also at Sylvia Plath's

"Mushrooms" and Philip Levine's "Animals Are Passing From Our Lives." Then write your own syllabic poem.

9. Do an *acrostic*, a poem in which you spell something down the left-hand side of the page; those letters then start each line of the poem. An example we like is Diane Wakowski's "Justice Is Reason Enough."

10. Invent rules that you then religiously, or not so religiously, follow: one sound per line; a poem that uses all the synonyms for "love"; a poem in which each stanza begins and ends with the same word. The point is to challenge yourself, to nudge your imagination in a potentially surprising direction.

Repetition, Rhythm, and Blues

Everything repeats. The seasons, the patterns of day and night, babies being born and parents dying, two people discovering each other's bodies: everything, large and small, has happened before — or almost. Nothing repeats itself in exactly the same way. Every moment is new: this day, this child, these pairs of hands and arms and eyes.

In our lives, we need both the comforts of repetition and the delights of change, and they need to be in balance. Too much repetition means a routine of dull habit, of closing out the world. Too much change, and we lose our center. The same principle applies to poems that use repetition.

Why say, in a poem, what you've already said? First, because it's pleasurable. We say "I love you" over and over to the people dear to us (or we should!). If you've just fallen head-over-heels for someone, you're likely to write their name from margin to margin in your journal, say it twenty times a day to yourself, and work it into every conversation until your friends are sick of it. Like good food and wine, words can be savored more than once.

And repeated words are powerful; they assert themselves, insist on our attention. Children know this: "Can I have some more? Please? Please please? Please please please please *please?*" In Catholicism, the repetition of prayers by the living is said to help reduce the time departed souls spend in purgatory. Buddhists repeat Sanskrit phrases to bring themselves in contact with the divine. Many peoples of the world have a long history of using repetitive chants and spells, prayers and invocations, to get the attention of the powers that be—to heal the sick, bless the crops or the marriage or the household, or to show their devotion. Poems partake of this tradition, too.

In the twentieth century, Gertrude Stein was the great literary repeater. She was fascinated with the possibilities and implications of reusing words, and did so—sometimes to the point of tedium. But her use of language was innovative, akin to what visual artists of the time were also exploring. For Stein, repetition was a way of subverting traditional ideas about what words were doing on the page. If the page was a canvas, maybe words could have the properties of paint—like color and texture—without having to refer to something else, to make meaning in the ordinary sense; they could live on the page *as words*, as themselves, just as an abstract painting is not a painting "of" anything; it's paint. As Stein said, "Rose is a rose is a rose is a rose."

Repetition as brushstroke, as incantation, as fundamental principle; it's basic to all poetry. Even when words aren't repeated, other things, like sentence structure or stanza patterns, may be. A traditional form like the sonnet is based on repeating rhythms and rhymes. The few subjects for poetry get recycled over and over again: love, death, loss, the self, the physical world, the world beyond it. All of it has been said before; all of it bears repeating, or we wouldn't be writing poems at all, but rereading.

There are two terms that might be useful to know: *repetend* and *anaphora*. *Repetend* is the irregular repetition of a word or phrase at various places throughout a poem. *Anaphora* is the repetition of a word or group of words at the *beginnings* of lines. Allen Ginsberg wrote many poems using anaphora, including his famous "Howl." His inspiration derived partly from Walt Whitman, who used repetition and long lines, while Whitman found *his* inspiration in the structure and repetition of Bible verses. A very different poet, Jane Cooper, uses the same strategies in this poem about grief:

LONG DISCONSOLATE LINES

in memory of Shirley Eliason Haupt

Because it is a gray day but not snowy, because traffic grinds by outside,
because I woke myself crying *help!* to no other in my bed and no god,
because I am in confusion about god,
because the tree out there with its gray, bare limbs is shaped like a lyre,
but it is only January, nothing plays it, no lacerating March sleet,
no thrum of returning rain,
because its arms are empty of buds or even of protective snow,
I am in confusion, words harbor in my throat, I hear not one confident
     tune,
and however long I draw out this sentence
it will not arrive at any truth.

It's true my friend died in September and I have not yet begun to mourn.
Overnight, without warning, the good adversary knocked at her door,
the one she so often portrayed
as a cloud-filled drop out the cave's mouth, crumpled dark of an old
     garden chair . . .
But a lyre-shaped tree? yes, a lyre-shaped tree. It's true that at twenty-four
in the dripping, raw Iowa woods
she sketched just such a tree, and I saw it, fell in love with its half-heard
     lament
as if my friend, in her pristine skin, already thrashed by the storm-blows
     ahead,
had folded herself around them,
as if she gave up nothing, as if she sang.

Cooper's repeated "because" in the first stanza immediately
engages our ear. "Because" is a word that usually explains, but here,
as the writer tells us, it explains nothing; behind that "because" is the
question, "Why?" The second stanza reveals one source of the narrator's confusion—the loss of her friend. Notice the repetition of other
key words—"nothing," "no," and "no" in the first stanza; "truth" at
the end of that stanza followed by "It's true . . . " in the opening of
the second. The image of the "lyre-shaped" tree is also repeated, leading us to that last line: "as if she gave up nothing, as if she sang." The

lyre is silent, the friend isn't singing, the poet can't find language that will "arrive at any truth." Yet the poem does arrive at a truth we recognize: poetry and art have limits, they're not enough, though they may be all we have.

If Cooper had used the word "because" to begin every line of her poem, the opening word would have grown predictable and stale. It is tricky sometimes to know when you're crossing the line, from hypnotic incantation to ordinary monotony. Repeating seems an easy and obvious technique, but it needs to be handled skillfully in order to be effective.

We're all familiar with *refrains* from popular songs—repeated lines that are often the "hook," lyrically and musically, which we're likely to remember later. Earlier forms of poetry, like ballads, which were originally sung, used a line or entire stanza as a refrain. Writers have found that refrains can still be memorable. Anne Sexton's "Ballad of the Lonely Masturbator" repeats the line, "At night, alone, I marry the bed." Galway Kinnell's long poem, "When One Has Lived a Long Time Alone," uses that line as a refrain at the beginning and end of each stanza of the poem. The word "alone" opens out to new experience and ideas each time, but afterward there's a return to the fundamental fact of the poet's situation. In both poems, the repetition is dynamic rather than static; it reinforces and emphasizes what the poet has to say.

When repetition is combined with rhythm—as it is in poetry and song—we pay attention and tune in. Robert Hass, in *Twentieth Century Pleasures*, talks about the basic way that rhythm is related to form. First there's the recognition of rhythm, the hearing of a particular pattern rather than random sounds. The next step is fooling around, making something pleasing or interesting—repeating, repeating, varying, repeating, exploring the possibilities. Finally, there's bringing it to some sort of closure. In music, a popular song has a melody, then a middle part called the bridge; afterwards it comes back to the melody again. That's one kind of form: statement, departure, a return that repeats the opening. A repeated rhythm can be as powerful—sometimes more powerful—than the words themselves. Rhythm is a bodily experience. It's the beat—whether of the conga drum, the bass guitar, or the stressed syllables in a line—that makes us not only listen, but long to dance.

Anne Waldman's "Fast Speaking Woman" is an example of a poem that explores repetition and variation exhaustively; it's hundreds of lines long. But a short poem can also make effective use of repeated rhythms and words. William Dickey wrote a series of chants, songs for the page that are brief but evocative. Here is one of them:

(*from* CHANTS)

5. The Lumber Company Executive

The sacred direction: down. Bring it to down.
Bring down these tents of assertion, the enemy,
the tall ones.

The sacred color: red. Bring it to red.
Wash down the widening gorges of earth flesh
till the stone stiffens.

The sacred instrument, fire. Bring it to fire.
Fire's afterbirth, the long dangle of waste, pitted
by unwilling waters.

The language of Dickey's poem might remind a reader of Native American chants and invocations: "the sacred direction," "the tall ones," "earth flesh," "fire." In this case the words are ironic, since the speaker is clearly against the earth, and the desire is to dominate rather than praise; the chant is profane. Each stanza begins with the repeated phrases "the sacred . . . " "Bring it to . . . " There's rhythmic repetition, too, even beyond those phrases; "BRING DOWN these TENTS of asSERtion" is echoed in the second stanza by "WASH DOWN the WIDening GORges." Each stanza's final line is shorter and has two stresses: "the TALL ONES"; "till the STONE STIFfens"; "the unWILLing WAters." All these elements, though we might not be aware of them on a first reading, unify the poem.

Here's the next piece from the series:

6. *The Critic*

I unscrewed the lip from the mouth, the mouth I discarded.
I unscrewed the lid from the eye, the eye I discarded.

Here is a doll made from pieces. The pieces hate one another.

Here are the doll and I in a posed photograph.
After the photograph was taken, I unscrewed the camera.

This is not exactly a flattering portrait; if we take the doll as symbolic of literature, the critic is the one who takes it apart, who destroys rather than creates. Notice the rhythms again: the first three lines each have a pause in the middle—a *caesura*—from a comma or period. Then there's the departure in the line, "Here are the doll and I in a posed photograph." The return to the familiar rhythm—longish line with a caesura the middle—adds to the sense of closure.

A form that uses repetition of both language and rhythm is the blues. As a song form, you're probably already familiar with it. The blues was born in this country, out of the sorrows of the black experience in America. Modern jazz and rock have their origins in the blues, but the blues never died, for many musicians and music lovers. It's also a form that poets have sometimes used to good effect. Langston Hughes, a black poet who became a major figure during the Harlem Renaissance of the twenties and thirties, wrote many jazz- and blues-influenced poems; in fact, he was the first writer to use the musical form of the blues as a poetic form. His first book was titled *The Weary Blues*. The blues has always been down-to-earth and personal, a lament about hard times—a cry of pain for love gone bad and no money in the bank and a cold world that just doesn't seem to care. The blues sings of those days when nothing goes right; it's a good form to try when you're feeling, well—blue. Here's a poem by Etheridge Knight:

A POEM FOR MYSELF

(or *Blues for a Mississippi Black Boy*)

I was born in Mississippi;
I walked barefooted thru the mud.

Born black in Mississippi,
Walked barefooted through the mud.
But, when I reached the age of twelve
I left that place for good.
Said my daddy chopped cotton
And he drank his liquor straight.
When I left that Sunday morning
He was leaning on the barnyard gate.
Left her standing in the yard
With the sun shining in her eyes.
And I headed North
As straight as the Wild Goose Flies,

I been to Detroit & Chicago
Been to New York city too.
I been to Detroit & Chicago
Been to New York city too.
Said I done strolled all those funky avenues
I'm still the same old black boy with the same old blues.
Going back to Mississippi
This time to stay for good
Going back to Mississippi
This time to stay for good —
Gonna be free in Mississippi
Or dead in the Mississippi mud.

If you've ever listened to a blues song, you could easily sing this poem. It opens with repeated lines, and then completes the beginning with a rhyme—in this case, "mud" gets rhymed with "good." Map out the pattern he's using for yourself, and then compare Knight's blues to a poem by Sandra McPherson:

BAD MOTHER BLUES

When you were arrested, child, and I had to take your pocketknife
When you were booked and I had to confiscate your pocketknife
It had blood on it from where you'd tried to take your life

It was the night before Thanksgiving, all the family coming over
The night before Thanksgiving, all the family coming over
We had to hide your porno magazine and put your handcuffs undercover

Each naked man looked at you, said, Baby who do you think you are
Each man looked straight down on you, like a waiting astronomer's star
Solely, disgustedly, each wagged his luster

I've decided to throw horror down the well and wish on it
Decided I'll throw horror down the well and wish on it
And up from the water will shine my sweet girl in her baby bonnet

A thief will blind you with his flashlight
                              but a daughter be your bouquet

A thief will blind you with his flashlight
                              but a daughter be your bouquet
When the thief's your daughter you turn your eyes the other way

I'm going into the sunflower field where all of them are facing me
I'm going into the sunflower field so all of them are facing me
Going to go behind the sunflowers, feel all the sun that I can't see

McPherson's poem looks different on the page, but it's essentially the same pattern as Knight's, with slight variations. In both poems, the repetitions emphasize both the music and the meaning. Knight describes the experience of a southern black boy, McPherson that of a mother with a troubled teenager; both poems sing different sorrows. Knight's language is closer to what we're used to hearing in the blues—"Said my daddy chopped cotton," "I been to Detroit and Chicago," "Said I done strolled those funky avenues." McPherson sometimes moves into language we would not expect, like "Solely, disgustedly, each wagged his luster."

A blues poem need not limit itself to particular subjects or language. You may want to follow the song form strictly, or alter it to suit your needs; you'll likely find that repetition of some sort is important to the idea of a blues, as well as a tone of sadness or complaint or loss. We poets always seem to have plenty of material in that area. But be forewarned: though it looks easy, a good blues poem is tough to write. If you're not careful, the constant repetition of words and rhythms can begin to sound dull or simplistic; that's the challenge of this particular form.

IDEAS FOR WRITING

1. Write a poem that uses anaphora. Use one or more of the follow-
   ing, which are guaranteed to trigger something interesting. Or
   invent your own.
   > I want
   > I remember
   > I used to
   > America
   > Love
   > Daddy
   > Mother
   > Give me back
   > You never

2. Using repeated words from the following list, write a chant that
   seems rhythmically interesting and has a sense of closure. Don't
   worry about what it means; just create something that feels complete. Let the words trigger the direction of the poem; you don't
   need to use all of them, and you can add as many words as you
   need.
   > smoke
   > angels
   > mirror
   > regret
   > moonless
   > pleasure
   > rose
   > glittering
   > face
   > oblivion
   > burning
   > strip
   > breaking
   > smolder
   > hotel

3. Do the preceding exercise with words you choose from a book of poems or fiction.

4. Write a short poem that begins and ends with the same line. The reader should feel differently about the line the second time he or she encounters it, because of what has happened in the poem.

5. Get yourself in the mood by listening to a few blues singers (we like Bessie Smith, Big Mama Thornton, Robert Johnson, Leadbelly, and Sonny Boy Williamson, to name a few). Then write your own blues poem, about something in your life that's getting you down. Or write a blues for a friend, your sister, Marilyn Monroe, or anyone else.

6. Steal a title from a blues song: "Empty Bed Blues," "Dead Shrimp Blues," "Honeymoon Blues," or anything else that appeals to you, and use it as a title for a blues poem of your own.

7. Write a poem with a refrain.

8. Write a poem with repetend.

9. Try repeating *images* in a poem: images of light, images of a certain color, images of things that are square, images of things that crawl—the possibilities are endless.

10. Take an old poem you wrote that does not use much repetition, and find words/images/rhythms/lines to repeat in it. Doing this might revitalize a poem that wasn't working.

More Repetition:
Villanelle, Pantoum, Sestina

We'd like to introduce you to three traditional forms that use repetition. The first is the *villanelle*, a French form which derived from Italian folk songs. A villanelle is a nineteen-line poem of five *tercets* (three-line stanzas) and a closing *quatrain* (four lines). Two lines in the poem get repeated throughout the entire poem, in a particular order; additionally, there's a rhyme scheme: the tercets rhyme aba, the quatrain abaa. If you map it out, it looks like this:

a1 (repeating line)
b
a2 (second repeating line)

a
b
a1

a
b
a2

a
b
a1

a
b
a2

a
b
a1
a2

As you can see, each line gets repeated alternately at the ends of the tercets; in the last stanza, the repeated lines get used one after the other. But the best way to grasp how villanelles work is to read some. Here's a lovely one by Martha Collins:

THE STORY WE KNOW

The way to begin is always the same. Hello,
Hello. Your hand, your name. So glad, Just fine,
and Good-bye at the end. That's every story we know,

and why pretend? But lunch tomorrow? No?
Yes? An omelette, salad, chilled white wine?
The way to begin is simple, sane, Hello,

and then it's Sunday, coffee, the *Times*, a slow
day by the fire, dinner at eight or nine
and Good-bye. In the end, this is a story we know

so well we don't turn the page, or look below
the picture, or follow the words to the next line:
The way to begin is always the same Hello.

But one night, through the latticed window, snow
begins to whiten the air, and the tall white pine.
Good-bye is the end of every story we know

that night, and when we close the curtains, oh,
we hold each other against that cold white sign
of the way we all begin and end. *Hello*,
Good-bye is the only story. We know, we know.

Collins's poem handles the requirements of the form beautifully. You'll notice that she doesn't repeat her lines exactly; the principle of variation we spoke of in the last chapter applies here, too. You have some flexibility in working out your poem, and one of the challenges and pleasures of this form is figuring out variations in your lines. You may want to repeat them exactly as you wrote them the first time, or you may find they need to be altered to fit with what's developing. *Developing* is an important concept here; you don't want to just repeat yourself, but to move the poem somewhere. Collins begins with the socially conventional, but as the poem unfolds, larger concerns emerge: beginnings and endings of relationships, and finally death, nonbeing, "that cold white sign / of the way we all begin and end." The knowledge at the end of the poem is the profound knowledge of our mortality. That's "the story we know," and it gets repeated, over and over.

One advantage of the villanelle is that once you settle on two good, interesting lines that you think will bear repeating—and that also rhyme—you've got much of the poem written. Just sit down, drop them into their slots, and fill in the blanks. (Remember that those middle lines of the tercets have to rhyme with each other, too.) Of course it's not as mechanical—or as easy—as that sounds. You may find you hate writing this way—or that you love it. But even if you don't produce a great villanelle, you'll get a sense of how they work. Some deservedly well-known villanelles you should look at are "One Art" by Elizabeth Bishop; "The Waking" by Theodore Roethke; and "Do Not Go Gentle Into That Good Night" by Dylan Thomas.

The *pantoum*, or *pantun*, is a form that a number of our students have taken to and really enjoyed. The pantoum is a Malayan form from the fifteenth century, and has its roots in Chinese and Persian poetry. Like the villanelle, the pantoum uses repeated lines. The pantoum is written in quatrains. The second and fourth line of each stanza become the first and third of the next. Usually, too, the first line becomes the last line, and the third line of the poem gets put into the very last stanza as the second line. Sound confusing? Once you have a first stanza, as in the villanelle, you can copy lines two and four into the next stanza as lines one and three, and you're in the midst of writing your poem. Again, you may want to repeat lines exactly, or to vary them as necessary.

In the following pantoum by Thomas Lux, notice how the lines are changed slightly so that the poem flows easily. We've seen much

more radical variations, even to the point of simply repeating only
one key word in what is supposed to be a repeated line. As always,
though, the principle is one of repetition, of echo.

ALL THE SLAVES

All the slaves within me
are tired or nearly dead.
They won't work for money,
not for a slice of bread.

Tired or nearly dead,
half underwater, wanting
merely a slice of bread:
the inner slaves, singing.

Half underwater, wanting
only a few flippers to swim,
the inner slaves, singing
the depth-charges within.

Only a few flippers to swim!
And a sensor to sense the sound
of the depth-charges within—
that's all they ask for aloud.

A sensor to sense the sound,
a hearer to hear the small aurals:
that's all they ask for aloud.
They're slaves with slaves' morals.

Hearers hearing small aurals,
they won't work for money.
They're slaves with slaves' morals,
all these slaves within me.

You might have noticed that Lux follows a rhyme scheme; this, too,
is part of the traditional pantoum's structure. Writers have felt free to
follow it or not, and to compose their own variations on the form.
Here's a pantoum by Linda Pastan, one which repeats the lines strict-

ly but varies the form slightly and doesn't rhyme. Instead of the first line being the last line, it ends up as the second line of the last stanza; the third line of the poem is the one that comes back at the end.

SOMETHING ABOUT THE TREES

I remember what my father told me:
There is an age when you are most yourself.
He was just past fifty then,
Was it something about the trees that made him speak?

There is an age when you are most yourself.
I know more now than I did once.
Was it something about the trees that made him speak?
Only a single leaf had turned so far.

I know more now than I did once.
I used to think he'd always be the surgeon.
Only a single leaf had turned so far,
Even his body kept its secrets.

I used to think he'd always be the surgeon,
My mother was the perfect surgeon's wife.
Even his body kept its secrets.
I thought they both would live forever.

My mother was the perfect surgeon's wife,
I still can see her face at thirty.
I thought they both would live forever,
I thought I'd always be their child.

I still can see her face at thirty.
When will I be most myself?
I thought I'd always be their child.
In my sleep it's never winter.

When will I be most myself?
I remember what my father told me.
In my sleep it's never winter.
He was just past fifty then.

This poem, haunted by the past, by the speaker's memory of her parents and her recognition of the cycles of life, finds its appropriate and moving expression in the repetition of the pantoum form. The third line, "He was just past fifty then," seems to resonate with heart-breaking significance as it closes the poem, informed as it is by all that's come before. The compelling back-and-forth movement of a pantoum lends itself to obsessive subjects—the mind going over and over particular events. It is also a good vehicle for expressing conflict, or ambivalence. Once you try this form, we think you may become an ardent convert, as several of our students have. We've seen successful pantoums on cocaine addiction, on divorce, on dieting, and even on O. J. Simpson.

Another interesting—and often maddening—form is the *sestina*, said to have been invented in Provence in the thirteenth century. The sestina doesn't repeat lines, only words. It consists of six stanzas of six lines each (*sestets*), and concludes with a final tercet. In the six stanzas, the end words get repeated in a certain order; in the closing tercet (called the *envoie* or envoy), all six words are used. If the six end words of the first stanza are labeled ABCDEF, the order of the words in each stanza goes like this:

1 ABCDEF
2 FAEBDC
3 CFDABE
4 ECBFAD
5 DEACFB
6 BDFECA

7 (the tercet): ECA for ends of lines; BDF in the middle of each line; that is, BE, DC, FA

What kinds of subjects are suited for a sestina? Interestingly, writers often feel compelled to write sestinas about writing sestinas! That's because this is truly a difficult one to pull off. Obsessions, compulsive desires, dreams, recurring events—these are good material for a sestina. Obviously you need to choose your six repeating words carefully, as these will sound throughout your poem, helping to create tone and mood and articulate your themes and ideas. We like what John Frederick Nims said about the form:

A shallow view of the sestina might suggest that the poet writes a stanza, and then is stuck with six words which he has to juggle into the required positions through five more stanzas and an envoy—to the great detriment of what passion and sincerity would have him say. But in a good sestina the poet has six words, six images, six ideas so urgently in his mind that he cannot get away from them; he wants to test them in all possible combinations and come to a conclusion about their relationship.

As with the repetition in a pantoum or villanelle, you have some leeway here, too. One trick writers have used is to substitute closely related words occasionally, instead of repeating them exactly: "here" might become "where," "two" become "to" or "too," "married" appear as "marriage" or even "marred." Coming up with creative solutions is part of the fun. Sometimes, too, poets will loosen the requirements— say, using all six words in the last tercet, but not following any order for where in the tercet they appear. Occasionally a writer will drop the concluding tercet entirely. In this sestina by Alberto Ríos, the six-line stanzas have been collapsed together, making two eighteen-line stanzas.

NANI

Sitting at her table, she serves
the sopa de arroz to me
instinctively, and I watch her,
the absolute mamá, and eat words
I might have had to say more
out of embarrassment. To speak,
now-foreign words I used to speak,
too, dribble down her mouth as she serves
me albóndigas. No more
than a third are easy to me.
By the stove she does something with words
and looks at me only with her
back. I am full. I tell her
I taste the mint, and watch her speak

smiles at the stove. All my words
make her smile. Nani never serves
herself, she only watches me
with her skin, her hair. I ask for more.

I watch the mamá warming more
tortillas for me. I watch her
fingers in the flame for me.
Near her mouth, I see a wrinkle speak
of a man whose body serves
the ants like she serves me, then more words
from more wrinkles about children, words
about this and that, flowing more
easily from these other mouths. Each serves
as a tremendous string around her,
holding her together. They speak
nani was this and that to me
and I wonder just how much of me
will die with her, what were the words
I could have been, was. Her insides speak
through a hundred wrinkles, now, more
than she can bear, steel around her,
shouting, then, What is this thing she serves?

She asks me if I want more.
I own no words to stop her.
Even before I speak, she serves.

Look at the words Ríos has chosen for his sestina: serves, me, her,
words, more, speak. These are the themes of the poem, too: the old
woman's life that has been spent serving others, the consideration of the
relationship between the narrator and nani, the concerns about language, and the "more" that is asked for and given. Nani's speech is of
two kinds—the "now-foreign" words that the narrator has lost, having,
we assume, grown up hearing and speaking them but learning English
in school; and the speech of her body, which is eloquently translated by
Ríos. The portrait is a compassionate one, detailing the quiet everyday
heroism of her life, and the cost of such selfless service. The simple
words, repeated throughout, accumulate their own quiet strength.

We once read a wonderful poem by Adam LeFévre, titled "Sestina Sestina—" one of those sestinas about sestinas. It concludes, "This form is a hungry monster. / Repetition wants something else every time. Six / mad kings and you, locked in a cell—that's a sestina." We couldn't resist concluding this chapter with one more sestina, that takes a different view—half-comically, half-seriously. The writer, Dana Gioia, pokes fun at sestinas and the students laboring over them; and, of course, he's written one in order to talk about it all.

MY CONFESSIONAL SESTINA

Let me confess. I'm sick of these sestinas
written by youngsters in poetry workshops
for the delectation of their fellow students,
and then published in little magazines
that no one reads, not even the contributors
who at least in this omission show some taste.

Is this merely a matter of personal taste?
I don't think so. Most sestinas
are such dull affairs. Just ask the contributors
the last time they finished one outside of a workshop,
even the poignant one on herpes in that new little magazine
edited by their most brilliant fellow student.

Let's be honest. It has become a form for students,
an exercise to build technique rather than taste
and the official entry blank into the little magazines—
because despite its reputation, a passable sestina
isn't very hard to write, even for kids in workshops
who care less about being poets than contributors.

Granted nowadays everyone is a contributor.
My barber is currently a student
in a rigorous correspondence school workshop.
At lesson six he can already taste
success having just placed his own sestina
in a national tonsorial magazine.

Who really cares about most little magazines?
Eventually not even their own contributors
who having published a few preliminary sestinas
send their work East to prove they're no longer students.
They need to be recognized as the new arbiters of taste
so they can teach their own graduate workshops.

Where will it end? This grim cycle of workshops
churning out poems for little magazines
no one honestly finds to their taste?
This ever-lengthening column of contributors
scavenging the land for more students
teaching them to write their boot-camp sestinas?

Perhaps there is an afterlife where all contributors
have two workshops, a tasteful little magazine, and sexy students
who worshipfully memorize their every sestina.

A Grammatical Excursion

To many people, even those interested in writing, "grammar" is a dirty word. It sounds stern, forbidding, and worst of all dull. It smacks of the elementary school classroom, of the meaningless dissection of sentences, of onerous burdens laid on the helpless shoulders of children. But if you are really interested in writing poetry, grammar can be something else: a door to rooms you might never otherwise discover, a way to realize and articulate your visions in language.

We asked a number of our students how they felt about grammar. Some were confident they knew their way around a sentence; many felt rusty, unsure whether they could remember much beyond the parts of speech. And others were downright terrified of the whole subject. Like fear of math, fear of grammar seems to be fairly common, rooted either in bad early experiences or an idea that such a mundane topic is deadly to creative inspiration. We can't do much about your third-grade teacher forcing you to diagram sentences, but we can tell you that a working knowledge of the sentence can be an invaluable tool for your development as a writer. If you were a serious musician, you'd know how to read music in both clefs. If you wanted to be a carpenter, you'd know the properties of various kinds of wood. A good chef knows what goes into a sauce, and what ingredients on hand might substitute in a pinch for something that's missing. This isn't to suggest that you couldn't play very well by ear, or learn how to make beautiful furniture by trial and error, or be a great instinctive cook. You may, in fact, already be writing luminous sentences without realizing it. But the odds are that solidifying your knowledge of grammar can enhance what you already know how to do; and odds are, too, that your sentences *aren't* as interesting, developed, and complex as you might make them.

Many books on creative writing are relatively silent on the subject of grammar. If you take a poetry workshop, you will hear elements of craft such as imagery and line being discussed; you may hear a teacher say something about "varying your sentences," or "using active verbs"—both generally good suggestions. But in all likelihood, you won't hear much discussion of how sentences work, of how, at the sentence level, you can begin to use certain grammatical structures to create richer detail, to develop your ideas, and to produce more sophisticated sentences. This is partly because the way that grammar has been taught in this country has undergone a change, relatively recently; it's only in the past few years that composition specialists have begun to explore more effective ways of doing it. Most of what they've discovered has been applied to teaching expository writing, but we think the methods could be just as useful for poets. If you study this chapter carefully, and practice the techniques in your own work, you'll see your language developing, achieving a greater flexibility and style.

We can't, in a single chapter, begin to cover what is after all a very large subject. So we're going to avoid technical terms as much as possible, and instead try to show you how to incorporate those "certain grammatical structures" we mentioned earlier—the ones that will do all those wonderful things for your writing. You should be familiar with the parts of speech: noun, pronoun, verb, adjective, adverb, preposition. If you're lost already, head for the dictionary or a basic grammar text, and be sure you know these terms. (Two good and unintimidating books for the grammar-shy are *The Transitive Vampire* and *Woe Is I.*) You might also find the following poem helpful. It was written for one of your authors, who can't keep the parts of speech straight—proving that you *can* be a poet and not know this stuff. But

since your other author has spent some time teaching it, she thought
she'd pass it on.

But first, the poem. It's not only a lesson in grammar, but a clever
villanelle—you should recognize the form from the previous chapter.

THE GRAMMAR LESSON

A noun's a thing. A verb's the thing it does.
An adjective is what describes the noun.
In "The can of beets is filled with purple fuzz"

of and *with* are prepositions. *The*'s
an article, a *can*'s a noun,
a noun's a thing. A verb's the thing it does.

A can *can* roll—or not. What isn't was
or might be, *might* meaning not yet known.
"Our can of beets *is* filled with purple fuzz"

is present tense. While words like *our* and *us*
are pronouns—i.e., *it* is moldy, *they* are icky brown.
A noun's a thing; a verb's the thing it does.

Is is a helping verb. It helps because
filled isn't a full verb. *Can*'s what *our* owns
in "*Our* can of beets is filled with purple fuzz."

See? There's almost nothing to it. Just
memorize these rules . . . or write them down!
A noun's a thing, a verb's the thing it does.
The can of beets is filled with purple fuzz.

—Steve Kowit

Now that we've got that straight—or slightly fuzzy—in our minds,
let's say that you want to write a poem about your grandmother. So
far you have the following lines:

My grandmother stands in the kitchen.
She sings the old songs. Her voice
rises and falls.

Is anything wrong with these lines? They're seemingly clear and direct. But in the writer's mind there are probably a number of images, memories, and ideas that haven't made it onto the page. Many beginning writers aren't aware that they've left most of what's in their head out of their poems. When you say "my grandmother" you see a person, vividly alive, unique, radiating all the things you love. All we readers see are the words "my grandmother." And what about "the kitchen"? You probably have a picture of that kitchen firmly in mind: how the light looks, the aromas, the sound of dishes being washed, where the kitchen table is, whether there are plants on the windowsill or curtains on the window. All three of these lines cry out for greater detail, for more information so that we as readers can experience what you, the writer, are trying to show us. It's possible that your poem could go on and tell us what we need to know in lines that will follow these; but let's say you want to do it here, in each of these sentences, to make them fuller and richer.

How can you say more about your grandmother and the kitchen, to make the scene come alive a bit? One way would be to add an *appositive* to each of these nouns. "Apposition" simply means that one thing is put beside another; an appositive is a word or group of words which explains the original in a little more detail. If you write "My grandmother, Stella," you have created a *noun appositive* for "my grandmother," since "Stella" is also a noun. Now we have a little more information; we know her name, at least. But you may want to tell us more, to use a group of words to describe her: "My grandmother, a tiny woman with long white hair and the face of a Botticelli angel." Now you've used a *noun phrase appositive*. (A *phrase* is a group of words.) You can also add an appositive to "kitchen": "the kitchen, a long, low room filled with the smell of grilling onions and roasting garlic." Now you can put them all together and even add one more appositive, something that tells us a bit more about that "smell of grilling onions" line:

> My grandmother, Stella, a tiny woman
> with long white hair and the face
> of a Botticelli angel,
> stands in the kitchen, a long low room

filled with the smell
of grilling onions and roasting garlic,
a smell I remember from childhood.

Now you've presented the scene in much greater detail than the original. We catch a glimpse of the grandmother, inhale the scent of her kitchen, discover something of the meaning that the image holds for the narrator of the poem—in a sentence which unfolds across seven lines.

From this small example, we hope you might begin to see some of the possibilities of using appositives. Appositives are a way to say more, to go further in the implications of your thought or the details of your memory or experience. They're a way of digging in, a process of discovery at the level of *syntax* (sentence structure).

For practice in recognizing appositives, here are some lines of poetry taken from several writers. The original word or phrase that's being added to is underlined, while the appositive (or appositives—sometimes there's more than one) is in italics. Notice how, in each case, the italicized language tells us *more*, extends and deepens and clarifies the writer's thought or image:

> They crowd <u>their rookery</u>, *the dilapidated outcrop*
> *The ocean gives a bubble-top of glass to at high tide.*
>
> —Mark Jarman,
> "Awakened by Sea Lions"

> I watch you watching the snake
> or gathering <u>the fallen bird</u>,
> <u>the dog in the road</u>, *those stiff bodies*
> *from whom you cannot withhold your tenderness.*
>
> —Ellen Bryant Voigt, "Rescue"

what, anyway,
was <u>that sticky infusion</u>, *that rank flavor of blood, that poetry,* by which
I lived?

> —Galway Kinnell, "The Bear"

> I've tried to seal <u>it</u> in,
> *that cross-grained knot*
> *on the opposite wall . . .*
>
> —Stanley Kunitz, "The Knot"

> What did you fear in <u>me</u>, *the child who wore*
> *your hair, the woman who let that black hair*
> *grow long as a banner of darkness . . .*
>
> —Marge Piercy, "My Mother's Body"

> <u>The body of my lady</u>, *the winding valley spine,*
> *the space between the thighs I reach through . . .*
>
> —Gary Snyder, "The Bath"

Not all appositives are nouns; verbs can be set beside other verbs, prepositional phrases beside other prepositional phrases, various kinds of clauses—noun, adjective, adverb—beside other clauses (a *clause* contains a subject and a verb, whereas a phrase doesn't). If we're confusing you, don't worry; though it's nice to know what an adverbial clause is, it's not really necessary. What's important is to be able to recognize similar structures, and then to work them into your own writing. Here, for example, are a few other kinds of appositives:

> On the tiles, the woman <u>whose throat</u>
> <u>is ringed with bandannas</u>, *whose collapse is a stain you want*
> *to step around.* (adjective clause)
>
> —Lynda Hull, "Gateway to Manhattan"

> . . . We moved
> <u>to the mountains</u>, *to a white house set into a notch*
> *above a shallow stream.* (prepositional phrase)
>
> —Charlie Smith, "Kohaku"

> it is not like <u>bringing a forest back</u>, *putting a truckload*
> *of nitrogen in the soil, burning some brush,*
> *planting seedlings, measuring distance—* (verbal phrases)
>
> —Gerald Stern, "The Shirt Poem"

Before we go any further, we want to give you a chance to practice some of these constructions. Following are some sample sentences; study them, and then complete the blanks with your own appositives.

(noun phrases)
MODEL: I wanted to return to <u>that place</u>, *the tiny fishing village in Mexico.*
YOUR SENTENCE: I wanted to return to that place, _____

_____

MODEL: I remember the <u>scent of my father</u>, *the cologne and cigarettes, the whisky on his breath.*
YOUR SENTENCE: I remember the scent of my father, _____

_____.

MODEL: I was thinking of <u>the soul</u>, *that body of light.*
YOUR SENTENCE: I was thinking of the soul, _____.

MODEL: <u>All that I love tonight</u>—*your body curled beside mine, the vase of white lilies, the one bird calling from the yard*—might be lost tomorrow.
YOUR SENTENCE: All that I love tonight— _____
_____— might be lost tomorrow.

(prepositional phrases)
MODEL: If you look <u>at the ugliness of the world</u>—*at the home-less woman lying in a doorway, at her dress of rags and bed of old newspapers*—you might see a kind of beauty.
YOUR SENTENCE: If you look at the ugliness of the world—
_____—you might see a kind of beauty.

MODEL: <u>After the funeral</u>, *after the flowers and eulogies,* we returned to our lives.
YOUR SENTENCE: After the funeral, _____, we returned to our lives.

(verbs)
MODEL: The seagulls <u>follow</u> the boat, *hover over the white wake.*
YOUR SENTENCE: The seagulls follow the boat, _____.

MODEL: The child <u>spins</u> in circles, *whirls around until the world spins with her.*
YOUR SENTENCE: The child spins in circles, _____.

MODEL: They <u>make love</u>, *touch the tenderest places, kiss the boundaries of skin.*
YOUR SENTENCE: They make love, _____.

(adjective clauses)
MODEL: You were the one <u>who took risks</u>, *who swam naked in the river, who laughed when the cops came.*
YOUR SENTENCE: You were the one who took risks, _____
_____.

(adjective phrases)
MODEL: The kitchen counter was <u>dirty</u>, *littered with cigarette butts, crowded with unwashed plates.*
YOUR SENTENCE: The kitchen counter was dirty, _____.

MODEL: She's <u>cautious</u>, *afraid to leave the house at night.*
YOUR SENTENCE: She's cautious, _____.

MODEL: The angels are <u>beautiful</u>, *luminous and full of longing.*
YOUR SENTENCE: The angels are beautiful, _____.

At this point we suggest—no, *insist*—that you take a break from this chapter. Don't read any further until you've had time to absorb everything we've covered so far. Read some other chapters. Write some poems. Do your laundry. Then, when you're ready, go back and reread the chapter up to this point, and practice more appositives until you're fairly comfortable with them. Take out some drafts of poems, look at your nouns, and see where the addition of some noun appositives would add greater detail. When you've got the hang of that, try other structures, such as the ones in the above sentences. Look for appositives in poems that you've read—yes, they're really there, lots of them. You'll quickly see that there are many more ways to expand sentences, and you may begin to feel confused. That's okay; the important thing is that you are beginning to look at poems *at the level of the sentence*, to pay attention to the parts, even if you can't name them. You'll find that, having studied even this much, the way you read poems will have changed. Changing your writing will take longer, and at first it may feel very awkward. Developing your syntax takes time. Keep reading, and practicing.

Okay. We assume you've taken our advice and been busy with other things, and are now ready for further punishment. Let's return to your original three lines about your grandmother and take the second one:

> She sings the old songs.

You could add an appositive to "songs," of course. But suppose it's not the songs you want to talk about, but the singing. Is there a way to do that? Try this:

> She sings the old songs, swaying back and forth,
> humming the parts she's forgotten, belting out
> the words she still remembers.

Now you've added three *verbal phrases* to your sentence. The verb is "sings," but that's not the only action taking place here. A *verbal* is a form of a verb, but it has no subject. Still, we know who's swaying, humming, and belting out the words: your grandmother. Verbals always have an *implied subject*: the subject of the sentence. So, if we were to break down the syntax here, it would look like this:

SUBJECT: She
VERB: sings
VERBALS: swaying, humming, belting out

You can do this with any action that's taking place, by simply adding an "ing" form of a verb. The first line of your poem could have been expanded with an "ing" verbal as well:

> My grandmother stands in the kitchen, *washing the dishes.*

or

> My grandmother stands in the kitchen, *wearing her plaid bathrobe.*

There are two other kinds of verbals: the "to" form, as in to wash, to shimmer, to love; and the "ed" form (sometimes "en"): bored, excited, driven. Here's how you could have expanded your second line with them:

> She sings the old songs
> *to remind herself of Russia.*
>
> *To comfort me,* she sings
> the old songs.
>
> *Exiled from her country,*
> she still sings the old songs.
>
> *Filled with her memories,*
> she sings the old songs.

Here are some examples of verbals in the work of other poets:

> . . . all her life
> She drank, *dedicated to the act itself . . .*
>
> —Lynn Emanuel, "Frying Trout While Drunk"

He'd been a clod, he knew, yes, *always aiming toward his vision of the good life, always acting on it.*

> —C. K. Williams, "Alzheimer's: The Husband"

> She washed the floor on hands and knees
> below the Black Madonna, *praying*
> *to her god of sorrows and visions . . .*
> —Lynda Hull, "Night Waitress"

> and the hawk hooked
> one exquisite foot
> onto a last thing
>
> *to look deeper*
> *into the yellow reeds*
> *along the edges of the water*
>
> —Mary Oliver, "Hawk"

For practice, try writing your own verbals, following the models below. Verbals, like appositives, don't always appear singly; you can string them together. In the above examples, C. K. Williams uses two. Try to use at least two verbals in each of your sentences. (The implied subjects of the verbals are underlined in each case.)

> MODEL: The cat sits before the window, *staring at the garden, anticipating the moment she'll be let out into it.*
> YOUR SENTENCE: The cat sits before the window, _____
> _____.
>
> MODEL: *Lurching down the street, smelling of cheap wine,* the man approached me.
> YOUR SENTENCE: _____, the man approached me.
>
> MODEL: *Exhausted, dispirited, temporarily defeated by the world,* you want someone to hold you.
> YOUR SENTENCE: _____, you want someone to hold you.
>
> MODEL: The boy studies his father *to remember him when he's gone, to fix his image forever in his mind.*
> YOUR SENTENCE: The boy studies his father _____
> _____.
>
> MODEL: *To love the world, to know it,* one wants to live long.
> YOUR SENTENCE: _____, one wants to live long.

By this point, you should have an idea of how you can expand your sentences and add detail to them with at least two kinds of grammatical constructions: appositives and verbals. In a well-written poem, many sentences will use these and/or other structures, sometimes repeating them, sometimes mixing them up. When structures are repeated, we call this *parallel structure.* (The King James translation of the Bible is full of it.) When you string together two or more appositives or verbals, you have parallel structure. When you make a list, you are creating parallel structure, too: "I love the *stars*, the *street-lights*, even the glittering *flecks* in the sidewalks." When you list a series of verbs—"The crow *lifts* its wings, *flies* to the highest branch of the maple tree, *regards* me without curiosity"—that, too, is parallel structure. The preceding "When . . . " sentence, and the two before it, are also an example; parallel structure doesn't just happen *within* sentences. By sensitizing your eye and ear to pick up on how sentences unfold, whether through the repetition of parallelism or the variation of different kinds of structures, you'll not only appreciate the writers you read at another level, but have a valuable tool for developing your own syntax. Here are some lines from poems in which appositives and verbals are used together:

> I watch the orderly stack the day's dead:
> men on one cart, women on the other.
> You sit two feet away, sketching
> and drinking tequila.
>
> —Ai, "Guadalajara Hospital"

Ai uses the appositives "men on one cart, women on the other" to tell us more about "the day's dead," making the description more graphic and disturbing. The action of the "you" in the poem is extended with the verbals "sketching" and "drinking." Bruce Weigl also presents his images in razor-sharp detail:

> . . . another soldier and I
> Lifted the shelter off its blocks
> To expose the home-made toilets:
> Fifty-five gallon drums cut in half
> With crude wood seats that splintered.
>
> —Bruce Weigl,
> "Burning Shit at An Khe"

The verbal "to expose" extends the action of lifting the shelter; the "home-made toilets" are described with an appositive, so that we can clearly see them. We can even almost *feel* those splinters from the wood seats.

Did Ai and Weigl set out to write sentences that used appositives and verbals in this way? Probably not. What's more likely is that they wanted intense imagery that would enable a reader to imagine those scenes. Ai knew that writing "You sit two feet away" wouldn't be enough; the verbals give us the sharp contrast of dead bodies against the seemingly casual activities of the other person. Weigl realized that "home-made toilets" wouldn't quite convey the memory of them to anyone who hadn't been there. In good writing, this is what happens. You have a sense, as you write and revise, of how to build your sentences so that they flow rhythmically, clearly, vividly. You aren't analyzing them as you go. If you are a pretty good tennis player, you aren't thinking "racket back, step forward, swing, follow through" as you rally; but in order to achieve that level, you probably spent some time practicing the motions, learning the component parts. Think of grammar in this way, too. It's hard going at first, but eventually can become second nature.

There's a lot more to grammar than we can possibly cover in one chapter. But we hope we've given you some options to explore in your own writing.

IDEAS FOR WRITING

1. Describe all the objects you see from a window in your house or apartment. That should give you lots of nouns; add appositives to them wherever possible, to describe them in greater detail. Let these descriptions trigger a poem about what these things mean to you, or let them remind you of some past incident or event which you include in the poem.

2. Observe an activity: a machine operating, a person doing something, the motions of an animal. Use verbals to capture everything that is happening. When you've captured the action as fully as possible, think about how that action could stand as a

metaphor for how you live your own life; how is the way you do things like the action you've described?

3. Make longer sentences out of the short ones that follow, using lots of sensual details so that a reader can vividly imagine the scene:
   The old man sat in the park.
   She was crying.
   He loved everything about the woods.
   I'm terrified of _____ . (Fill in a word or words to describe your fears, and go on.)
   It was a beautiful day.

4. Take a draft of a poem and study your sentences. Do they tend to follow a similar pattern? One common problem is static syntax—the same thing, over and over. Many people fall into a repetitive subject–verb construction: "I shot the bear. The bear died. I left it there in the snow. I headed home. My father sat there reading the paper. He asked what had happened. I told him." This can be an effective strategy sometimes, if used deliberately and not unconsciously. If this is your pattern, start fooling around and seeing what you can add to each sentence. Remember that idea of repetition and variation: if you have a lot of long sentences, break them down into short ones occasionally.

5. Take another draft of a poem and underline all the adjectives. Are there a lot of them? Do you tend to load them up before the nouns? Cut out as many as possible. See if there are other ways to describe things without using adjectives. (Another trick: put the adjectives *after* the noun; instead of "my frail weak grandfather lies in his bed" try "my grandfather—frail, weak—lies in his bed.")

6. Write a poem which is *one* long sentence. Make it at least twenty lines.

7. Write a sentence in which you withhold the subject and verb as long as possible; that is, begin with a preposition, or an adverb, and pile up the phrases and clauses.

8. Write a poem which uses a lot of parallel structure. Any time you do something, try and repeat it, to the point of obsession and probably comedy. Then, when you've pushed it as far as you can, go back over it and cut out what you need to in order to make it a good poem.

The Energy of Revision

> The energy of revision is the energy of creation and change,
> which is also the energy of destruction.
>
> —Maggie Anderson

Revision is the poet's most difficult, demanding, and dangerous work. Difficult because it's hard to let go of our original inspirations or ideas or our best lines, as we may have to do in the service of the poem. Demanding because it calls for us to reach deeper or further than we may want to, or feel we know how to. Dangerous because we feel we might, in the act of trying to make a good poem better, lose touch with the raw energy that drove the poem into its fullness to begin with and destroy what we have so joyously created. But revision is necessary work for poets who care about their craft. Richard Tillinghast, in an essay titled "Notes on Revision," says, "The willingness, the ardent desire even, to revise, separates the poet from the person who sees poetry as therapy or self-expression." Ardent desire may be a bit more than we can hope for, but certainly willingness is important.

A student once asked us why critique workshops are so "amputory" in nature, why they seem interested only in cutting away from the poem. Editing is one of the easiest and fastest routes to rewriting, simply because it's often much easier to identify something that doesn't belong: a cliché, an unnecessary adjective, a confusing or misplaced word, line, stanza or image. It's more expedient to get rid of what's not working than to figure out how to make it work. Similarly, a poem often opens with unnecessary lines—a kind of "throat-clearing," as one of our students called it—before the true poem begins. Another problem is that of going on long after your poem has ended. A good workshop can help point these things out to the writer.

It's much more difficult to see where or how a poem might be opened up, where a wrong turn has been taken, what's missing. A workshop should focus on these things, too, and try to illuminate as many possible avenues of development as its members can think of, so that the poet has a variety of options. Sometimes workshops are limited in that they may not always have quite enough time for a thorough examination and contemplation of the poem. A workshop should be considered a starting point for revision, a place where you can begin to gather ideas about what you need to do to make the poem what it wants to be.

True revision is just that: a re-visioning of the poem's potential and the strategies it has used so far. In an early draft, the language on the page should be considered temporary language, ripe with possibilities, with the gifts your subconscious mind has offered up. In the act of getting down a first or second or fourth draft, you're likely to have tapped into not only some raw, pure, evocative language but also a lot of received language and attitudes—clichés, easy solutions, awkward phrasing, habitual ways of articulation, vague generalities. Sometimes your ego or your editor has gotten in the way, and tried to make things too pretty, or too petty; maybe irony has stepped in where sincerity was needed, or vice-versa. Maybe you've been melodramatic in an attempt to be powerful, or sentimental when you wanted deep feeling. Maybe the poem is unfocused, with too many incidents, too confused a sense of what it's about, or no sense at all. The true poem, in other words—the one you wanted to write, the inspiration that got you feverishly tapping out lines on the computer at three a.m.—may not yet have found its realization on the page.

If you consider what you've written in the early stages as pointing toward the true poem, rather than being the poem itself, it will be easier for you to be open to what still needs to happen for it to succeed.

The more willing you are to let go of your own words, to demand more of your language and push your limits to get to something better, the more likely it is that you will eventually produce a worthwhile poem. There's nothing wrong with "shitty first drafts," as Anne Lamott calls them in her book on writing, *Bird by Bird*. Every writer produces garbage—stupid, embarrassing, awful stuff. If you truly want to write well, you have to be willing to see when you've written badly, and keep trying to improve on what you've done.

Another question we are often asked is: How do I know when my poem is finished? Three drafts? Ten? Fifty? We can't give you a number. Some poems arrive fairly whole and need little work, others may come to you in fragments over a period of time, others may need reworking for months before you even begin to see results. The famous formulation is that a work of art is never finished, merely abandoned. One of the ways to abandon a poem is to send it out for publication. If it's published, is it finished? Maybe, though sometimes just the act of typing up the final draft to send out, seeing the poem objectively for a moment, through the eyes of a possible publisher, may lead to a last-minute revision. Even poems that are published may be in need of further work. We've seen several in magazines that we wish the writer had given one more critical pass. The painter Bonnard would actually go to museums and galleries where his paintings hung, sneak in, and rework his canvases. Revision is a process that has no clear ending point. A poem is like a child; at some point we have to let it go and trust that it will make its own way in the world.

Can you revise a poem too much? How much is too much? Sometimes, in our fervor to revise, to get it right, we can end up editing the life out of a poem. We know we're on dangerous ground here to tell you that poems can be overrevised, because in fact, what's more common is an unwillingness to revise enough. However, it can and does happen. If you find yourself losing interest in a poem, if it begins to look pale and wan, corpse-like, it's time to bury it for a while; throw it into a drawer, along with each draft, and leave it alone. Return to it in a week, a month, a year. Come back to it with new eyes, new knowledge. When you do, it may be easier to see what's working and what isn't. (If you still find it difficult to part with those "golden lines" you know are brilliant but have no place in the poem, save them in a box labeled "great stuff.")

If you keep a journal like we do, chances are that most of what can be found there is pure junk: notes, diatribes, meanderings. But once in a while something begs to be let out of the journal and onto the printed page, saying *I think I could be a poem.* The simple process of transferring the journal entry onto the typewriter or computer is often the beginning stage of revision; that's when line breaks are usually begun, when you might add or delete a section, reconstruct an image or phrase, play with the music of a hastily written line. See, you've already begun and it wasn't that painful. However, once the "poem" is arranged into some sort of agreeable shape, the real work begins. Since it's hard to be objective about your own work, it's helpful, when you feel you've taken the poem as far as you can on your own, to get further reactions from a teacher or workshop or trusted reader—one who knows something about poetry. Ideally, such a reader, or readers, will send you back to the poem with fresh ideas for developing it.

Sometimes, though, you get to a point where you're stuck. You know the poem isn't working, but you can't seem to get anywhere with it. Maybe you've had some contradictory suggestions—one person loves a stanza, another person has drawn a big "x" over it and handed it back. Feeling confused, demoralized, ready to burn your poem, or perhaps your critics—these are common reactions at this stage. As we said, it usually helps to leave the poem alone, let the dust settle, and come back to it after some time has passed. If you're still stuck, here are some tips on how to tackle the poem again.

1. *Turn the poem over and start again.* Rewrite it in lines or a freewrite, but cover the same experience/event/idea. Feel free to change, add to, or go in a different direction from the original.

2. *Change the way your poem looks on the page;* you won't be able to help changing some language as well. You might alter line length, stanza breaks, flush-left margins, poem length, punctuation, capitals.

3. Take any problematic line in your poem and *rewrite it at least*

five ways. Don't just substitute one word for another—i.e., "skin" for "flesh"—though that might be part of it. But change, as well, the syntax of the line.

4. Some poems start out well, but then veer off on the wrong track. *Find your wrong turn* and go in a completely different direction— even the opposite one. Rewrite the poem from that point on, ignoring where you ended up before.

5. *If the poem has a controlling metaphor, try changing it.* If you've written a poem about falling in love as drowning in an ocean, try reimagining the experience as climbing a mountain or taking a train ride or finding a twenty on the sidewalk.

6. *Write a question word*—How, Why, When, What, Where, Who—in the margin where *answering* that question will help you develop further.

7. *Try surgery*—the "amputory" method. You can also think of it as weeding the garden of your poem. Lop off the beginning and/or the end. Or, cut 3–5 lines to see if you really need them.

8. Shake up the poem and *break whatever pattern you've developed.* Look at: point of view; syntax; imagery; adjectives; and anything else you can think of.

9. *Radical surgery:* Find the heart, the core of your poem— whether it's one line, or an image, or a statement—that is is the essence of what the poem wants to be about. (If you can't find such a line, try writing one.) Now forget the rest of the poem: use that one great statement/image/line and write a new poem that lives up to it.

10. If nothing seems to be working, and you've really tried, put the poem away in a folder that says "In Process." Then—yes, we'll say it a third time—*leave it alone.* Every so often, go back and try again.

Poet Jane Hirshfield has thought a lot about the more existential aspects of revision. Reprinted here is a worksheet she handed out to her students at the Napa Valley Writers' Conference.

Some Possible Questions to Ask of Your Poem in Revision

What is being said?

Is there joy, depth, muscle, in the music of its saying?

Is there more that wants to be said?

Does it want a more deeply living body of sound?

Is it true?

Is it ethical?

Does it feel?

Does it follow its own deepest impulses, not necessarily the initial idea?

Does it know more than you did when you started it?

Are there things in it that don't belong?

Are whatever digressions it takes in its own best service?

Are there things in it that are confusing?

Are there things in it that are clichéd or sentimental?

Is it self-satisfied?

Is it predictable?

Does it go deep enough? far enough?

Is it particular?

Is the grammar correct?

If the syntax is unusual, is it for a purpose?

Are the transitions accurate?

Is it in the right voice?

Is it in the right order?

Does the diction fit?

Could any of its words be more interesting? more surprising? more alive?

Do its rhythms work? (i.e., both seem right and accomplish meaning and feeling)

Does the music work?

Does the shape/form work? (line breaks, stanzas, etc.)

Does each image work? each statement?

Does it allow strangeness?

Does each of its moments actively move the poem toward its full realization?

Should it go out into the world?
Is it a seed for something else?
Is it finished?
Six months later, is it still finished?
Six years later, is it still finished?

Some of these questions may never get answered to your satisfaction. But they can provide a useful starting point for rewriting. Not all your revisions will become successful poems, but that doesn't matter; you'll have learned more about language, and your own process, and that knowledge will carry over into other poems and help you solve their particular problems. So don't despair, however hard it may seem to go back to that poem one more time. Finally getting it right will be worth everything it took to get there.

THE WRITING LIFE

Self-Doubt

We work in the dark—we do what we can, we give what we have.
Our doubt is our passion and our passion is our task. The rest is
the madness of art.

> —Henry James

> There is in you what is beyond you.
> —Paul Valéry

The thing that usually gets me through the writing is that my feelings of wretched inadequacy are irregularly punctuated by brief
flashes of impotence.

> —James L. Brooks

In writing, as in other endeavors, there are times when you don't feel
equal to the task before you. Every great and not-so-great writer has
suffered bouts of feeling worthless, lazy, untalented, mediocre, and
boring. Sylvia Plath, a brilliant poet, tormented herself with such
doubts. Read her *Journals* and you'll discover passages like the following:

> Can I write? Will I write if I practice enough? How much should
> I sacrifice to writing anyway, before I find out if I'm any good?
> Above all, CAN A SELFISH EGOCENTRIC JEALOUS AND
> UNIMAGINATIVE FEMALE WRITE A DAMN THING
> WORTHWHILE?

In entry after entry, Plath exhorted herself to become a better person, to take more detailed notes on the lives around her so she could turn them into fiction (which she considered the "real work"), to write articles, read more books, work harder, improve her teaching, and on and on, relentlessly, destructively pushing herself to realize an ideal of perfection she could never attain. At the age of thirty she committed suicide, leaving a body of work that culminated in the stunning poems of *Ariel*. What a loss, of all she might have lived and written afterwards.

Many of us tend to focus more on our failures than our successes. But doing so ensures that you will always doubt your abilities and talents, since you can always point to some incident that "proves" you're no good. In the literary life, which is full of rejected manuscripts, lost awards and prizes, and critical judgments of your work, it's essential to develop some self-appreciation—to delight in your successes, wherever and however they arrive. If your workshop praises a poem, don't think everyone is too nice to tell you how terrible it really is. (If it *is* that kind of workshop, you should get out of it as soon as possible—honest feedback is the sign that people respect your writing and take it seriously.) If a journal publishes your work, don't assume the editors have bad taste. If you win an honorable mention in a contest, realize that your poetry stood out as worthier than that of many others; don't obsess over not winning first or second prize. Poetry, ultimately, is not a competition, in spite of the competitive nature of achieving publication and recognition. If you see it as such, you're likely to feel unhappy, instead of being nourished by it.

Another point is worth mentioning here: You are not your poetry. Your self-esteem shouldn't depend on whether you publish, or whether some editor or writer you admire thinks you're any good. If you write a poem about something that happened to you, and a critic trashes the poem, don't take it personally. We've seen this over and over: people equate their self-worth with their poetry. They're crushed by rejection, by criticism. They wonder what's wrong with them, why they're no good. Or they blame a teacher, an editor, a fellow student, and they stew with resentment. The truth is that good poems come from a combination of things: awareness, talent, persistence, persistence, native and acquired language abilities, luck, persistence, knowledge, imagination, persistence . . . None of these qualities necessarily makes one a good human being, though we'd like to believe that poets are somehow more noble than other folks. But poets are people who happen to have a particular relationship to language, a strong need and desire to use it in a certain way. Poets, as people, may be selfish, callous, opportunistic, manipulative, unstable, irresponsible—or the opposite. Who you are contributes to your poetry in a number of important ways, but you shouldn't identify with your poems so closely that when they are cut, you're the one that bleeds.

We know a writer who insists he's no good. He's published several fine novels and books of short stories, had a couple of television scripts produced, and has won many awards. There's simply no correlation between how he feels about his work and the luminous fact of his prose, but there it is. It's painful to see this in someone else, painful to confront it in yourself. You feel you don't have enough talent, or that you started too late, or will never have the skill to say what you want to in the right way. You wonder if you're wasting your time; you're sitting alone in a room when you could be out living your life. You think about how no one reads poetry, how no one will care whether or not another poem comes into the world. You must be a masochist to even consider writing poems. This book you're reading was a waste of money; why did you buy it, what the hell made you think you could write? None of this negativity has a thing to do with whether you're going to be able to write a poem, unless you let it get the upper hand and keep you from the blank page. If you want to write poems, you have to acknowledge that that's what you want to do, and quit sabotaging yourself. Don't give in to doubt; feel it, recognize it, and then quit beating yourself up and get to work.

Here's an exercise we sometimes give to our students: Sit down and let that nagging, negative voice have its say. Catalog your faults, your limitations, all the reasons you can't write, every inner and outer obstacle you can think of; convince yourself, on paper, that you will never be a writer.

Now give yourself a chance to answer that voice. Tell it why you want to write, and what you intend to write about; tell it how wonderfully creative you are, and believe it. Find that positive place inside of you that is at the heart of your desire to write. What is that place all about? Maybe it's the memory of stories your parents read to you as a kid, their magical quality. Maybe it's the pleasure you get from reading poems that resonate with your own life, that articulate things you've felt or experienced, or simply dazzle you with the sensuous quality of the language. Maybe it's the satisfaction you feel when you get down exactly what you need to say, striking just the right tone. And what about the freedom of roaming through your imagination to record whatever occurs to you, and to create whole worlds where you can play God and make things happen that you will never actually experience? In your writing you can make love to whoever you want. You can talk to the dead, relive your childhood, cancel the bad debts of regret. You can become a stripper, or a stone in a river. You can steal, murder, fall in love, change the outcome of history or of a conversation you had the day before. Whatever that place in your imagination is about, describe it to that other part of yourself that wants to spoil your fun.

You can do this exercise, not just once, but whenever you want to pull yourself out of the muck of self-doubt. Use it as therapy, or as a warmup to get yourself writing when you feel blocked, or to generate some raw material that might turn into a poem.

Writer's Block

NOT WRITING

A wasp rises to its papery
nest under the eaves
where it daubs

at the gray shape,
but seems unable
to enter its own house.

—Jane Kenyon

All of us have felt this way at one time or another, as if we had been
banished from the kingdom of our own feelings, thoughts, words. It
helps to know that we aren't alone in this. But here's the good news:
We don't believe in writer's block. We believe there are times when
you are empty and times when you are full. When you're full to over-
flowing you write poems until you're empty, then you wait around
while you get filled up again. You can help fill yourself up with stuff:
books of poetry, novels, movies, new kinds of food, travel, relationships, art, gardening, TV, school, music . . . basically, experiences.
And while you're doing that, your life will fill you up with all that you
can't control: the death of a friend, unexpected moments of intense
joy, car accidents, births, natural disasters, spring, war, dental surgery,
phone calls from old lovers. Once you have enough of those under
your belt you can write again. In the meantime, relax and write what-

ever you can, even if it has that empty feeling, and wait until your head clears and you're full. When you are, the passion will be back, and the poems. That much said, we want to emphasize the importance of writing through those stretches of emptiness. The poetic mind is a muscle that needs exercise to stay in shape. If you were preparing for a big race you wouldn't sit around for weeks beforehand munching burritos. Well, the big poem is coming your way and you need to prepare. Here are some exercises you can do while you're waiting for the muse to raise the green flag.

1. *Keep a journal and write in it every day*, even if it's only for ten minutes. What most writers lack in abundance is time. Our lives are so busy. There are so many things that need to get done in a day and they are all much more important than writing a poem. But think of it this way: if a good friend called you and said, "I know you're busy, but can I have ten minutes of your time?" you'd probably oblige and settle in for fifteen. We all have a few minutes a day we can spare for something we care about. It's a reasonable amount of time. Give yourself ten minutes a day and don't just wait for it to appear. If you drink coffee in the morning and stare out the window for half an hour, give yourself twenty minutes to stare and ten minutes to write. Or ten minutes before you go to sleep, or ten minutes around lunch time. Figure out a time during the day that you generally have to yourself and mark it in your calendar. Make a date with yourself. Now you want to know, What do I write about? Keep it simple. Write down an image that struck you the day before, or one from memory. Expand on it for a few minutes. Or write down a number of images, briefly: the boy at the gas station, the stunted tree in the backyard, the man who dropped his suitcase at the airport, notes for possible poems. This is "no fault" writing. It doesn't have to be good, it just has to get done. Think of it as a program to get you back on track. Do it for ten days and see what happens. We've tried this ourselves and always with good results. We've looked through our journals and found that when we put ourselves on this ten-day program, we inevitably ended up with something that could be called a poem. Remember, writing begets writing.

2. If you can't seem to bring up any images and you're the kind of person who sits down with pen and paper and finds yourself catching up on your correspondence in order to feel like you're "getting something done"—really just another maneuver to avoid writing a poem—*write someone a postcard or a letter in the form of a poem*, thereby getting two things done at once.

3. *Discover the things you do to avoid writing and make them work for you.* If your eye and mind tend to wander, simply look up from your desk and describe whatever is in your field of vision—an object in the room, the view from your window; or look down and describe your shoes or your bare feet. If you tend to talk on the phone with friends, write down what you'd say to a friend in a phone call. Make a list of every little thing you *should* be doing, and turn that list into a poem.

4. If that fails, *write about why you can't write.* Make a list of excuses, a list of the subjects you can't write about or feel you shouldn't write about and why, a list of all the things that haven't happened to you yet, places you haven't been, the books you haven't read and want to or feel you should. Feel sorry for yourself, call yourself names, get angry at all those who keep you from writing (there's nothing like a little invective to get the juices flowing). Do this for ten days, ten minutes a day. See what happens.

5. If you still find yourself staring at the blank page for the full ten minutes, fine. You've still done your work. Do it again tomorrow and the next day and the next, stare at the blank page and *don't write a single word for ten days.* See what happens—we bet you won't be able to keep yourself from writing.

6. If you work more effectively with others or need extra support and motivation, *try writing with a friend.* Make a date with another recalcitrant poet or meet at a coffee house or in the park. Synchronize your watches and write for ten minutes. Then do what you want; go for an ice cream, a movie, whatever. Guilt-free. You've done your work for the day.

7. There are other ways to kick the habit of not writing. *Go to a reading.* A good reading has often sent us home filled again and ready to write. Or, *set up a reading for yourself.* Call a bookstore or cafe which regularly hosts writers, or attend an open mike and sign up. It's great motivation for looking closely at your poems, doing some revision, or even writing a new poem.

8. *Take a vacation from your habitual work spot.* Get away for awhile, even if it's only for the weekend or the day. Even a change of a few hours can help. If you always write in your kitchen, bedroom, office, go to a coffee shop or park. Go on a bus or train ride and don't take along a book; bring your notebook and pen.

9. *Look through your old journals and notebooks* and see what you wrote when you "used to write." When in your life did you write regularly and well; where were you, what were you doing, how did you feel, what made you feel that way? Perhaps you write better when you're depressed, and now you're so happy you can't get a word down. Or perhaps the opposite is true. Either way, recognize that something will change. It's the one thing you can count on.

10. *Take a workshop or go to a writers' conference.* Put yourself in a position where you're challenged to write and to think of yourself as a writer. A weekly group can help push you to organize your time so you'll get some writing done. Another benefit is meeting others who share the same concerns and difficulties. A writers' conference can be a brief but intense time to refuel yourself with daily readings, lectures, discussions, and workshops. A good conference with a lively and inspirational group of teacher/poets can recharge your batteries for the entire year. Look in magazines like *Poets & Writers* to find listings for conferences around the country.

So that's our program. We don't guarantee great poems, but we do guarantee that you'll *write*, which is where every great poem begins. Pulitzer Prize-winner Carolyn Kizer once told a story about those poems that come to us as "gifts," the ones we don't have to struggle over. Kizer was working on a long poem for weeks, unable to make much headway, feeling frustrated and blocked. She kept at it long after she felt she should give up. One morning she sat down at her desk with the poem in front of her, ragged and misshapen as ever, and she was suddenly struck by inspiration and wrote a new poem which came quickly and fully. The way she explained it, the muse saw her struggling, determined and committed for days on end and then decided, out of the goodness of her heart, to give her a poem, *gratis*. And of course the poem wasn't really free; Kizer had worked hard for it and was entitled to the fruits of her labor. The poem only *felt* free, but what a feeling.

Writing in the Electronic Age

Only a few years ago, we knew several writers who didn't have computers. They were nervous about technology, or figured they could get by for a while without investing the money, or insisted that they couldn't create without the typewriter they'd been using for years. We still know a few writers like this. They labor over drafts, typing and retyping, Liquid Paper staining their shirts. They drive to the copy center when they could be laser printing hard copies in their kitchen.

Computers aren't everything, of course. You might prefer the feel of a pen in your hand, or like to bring your journal to a cafe or into bed with you as you write out ideas, memories, scraps of conversation. If you're used to longhand, switching to a keyboard might not make your thoughts flow more easily. But when you want to rewrite, to get your poem ready to show your writer's group or class or a potential publisher, the computer is a godsend. It saves time. It frees you from some of the drudge work, so you can capture your thoughts more quickly, rearrange them, take them out of silence and into form. Most writers have realized these advantages, and most now happily work on computers, or at least word processors.

But computers are just the starting point; now there's the Internet, a worldwide network of computer systems, and the World Wide Web, a graphical interface and global hypertext system. The writer sitting alone at her desk, staring at her PC or Macintosh screen, might be contemplating a difficult draft. But she just as easily might be talking to other writers in London or Saipan, or perusing the notebooks of Walt Whitman in the Library of Congress, or getting some feedback from an online teacher. She might be conducting an e-mail correspondence with the editor of a literary journal about her work, or posting a few poems on her Web home page for any of millions of potential viewers. She might be searching a database for information on Dante, down to a particular canto and line in his *Divine Comedy*, or listening to the recorded voice of George Plimpton, editor of the *Paris Review*, welcoming her to the journal's Web site. She might even be writing—but not in the usual way. Now there's hypertext fiction and poetry—nonlinear, interactive work which can involve a number of authors, or a number of ways through a text that can be determined by the person reading it. She might be mixing sound, images, and even video with the words onscreen.

Clearly, the world writers live in is changing. Things on the Internet are happening with such dizzying rapidity that a good part of the information in this chapter could be out of date by the time you read this. By the time we finish writing this sentence, three new poetry sites will have been launched on the Web. Not only businesses are rushing into cyberspace in what's been called an electronic Gold Rush; writers and artists of all kinds are also staking their claims. The creative potential is just as large as the commercial possibilities, and many who are passionate about literature are logging on to share that passion and explore the wealth of opportunities for reading, writing, publishing, and networking with people all over the world.

The implications of what's happening now are staggering for those of us who have been readers of books and want to be writers of them. The book itself—printed on paper pages, bound, published, and shipped to a warehouse, put on the shelves of a store and taken home—such a book may eventually be a collector's item, akin to a box of record albums. Remember 45s? How about 78s? Still have those 33-1/3s left over from the eighties? They're probably warping and gathering dust, shoved behind your CD collection. Right now, you can buy CD-ROMs of Dickens, Twain, Shakespeare, and countless others. CD-ROMs have been coming down in price, so they're worth checking into; you can get collections of poetry, science fiction, contemporary novels, literary magazines, screenplays, and almost anything else you can think of, all with searchable databases for easy reference. (See Appendix D, "More Resources For Writers," for some suggested CD-ROMs.) On the Internet, you can download Homer's *Odyssey* and William Strunk's 1918 classic *The Elements of Style* without moving from your desk. According to an article in *Poets & Writers* magazine, there will eventually be a computer the size of a paperback, with a screen as readable as the printed page, so you can take along something to read at the beach or the laundromat. We don't know if such technologies are going to take the place of the book, but they're definitely important.

Whether all this sounds scary or exhilarating—or a bit of both—being a poet in the twenty-first century is going to be different from what it has been in the twentieth. The very way we read poems and take in their meaning may change radically. Reading a poem on the page is a different experience from seeing it on a screen, where clicking on a highlighted word might refer you to a definition or to some historical background, or where another click might lead to the poet's biography or to related works by other authors, or to a video of the actual poet discussing the work's origins and structure. You might click on lines the poet has revised, to read alternative versions of the poem. Channel-surfing through a text alters, for better or worse, our experience of it.

The new technologies have other implications as well. There is increased access to a community of other writers and literary folk. It's difficult, when you're starting out, to make such connections, but the Internet offers immediate contact with likeminded souls around the world. It also offers access to information about publishing, contests, literary theory, writers' biographies, and obscure or hard-to-find books that aren't likely to be widely available. Finally, the Web is democratic. Anyone can put up a Web page and "publish" poems for a potentially large audience, without an editor or agent or book contract.

If you don't have a modem—we're assuming you have a computer—you should seriously consider getting one. They're inexpensive, and a number of online services offer reasonable enough rates. Getting connected can take a bit of work—you have to figure out how to get your modem talking to your Internet service provider—but the rewards are well worth it. If you own a Macintosh, there's an Internet Starter Kit with a book and disks available to help you. And most service providers offer technical support and advice, if you don't happen to have a close friend who's wired and knowledgeable about the online world. Also, the formats are getting simpler all the time, so that even the biggest technophobe needn't fear being lost in cyberspace. In fact, getting online may be easier than, say, figuring out how to program a modern VCR. If you live in an area where there are few writers and fewer good bookstores, a modem and Internet service provider can make the difference between being isolated and being part of a worldwide community that can offer support, information, and inspiration.

There are so many online resources for poets right now that we could fill a book with what's available. Big commercial Internet service providers such as America Online have a variety of offerings; America Online, for example, hosts an Author's Cafe, a chatroom where you can talk in real-time with other writers, both well-known and aspiring. Here in the San Francisco Bay Area, the WELL is a local provider very popular with writers. When considering an online service, you'll want to check out not only the cost for monthly charges and actual time online, but what sorts of special features, unique to that provider, are offered. All of them should give you access to the Internet, and enable you to e-mail and browse the World Wide Web.

Internet service providers will also give you access to Usenet Newsgroups—electronic bulletin boards—some of which are focused on books and writing. There, people might post anything from personal questions about a favorite author to arguments about literary theory. "Rec.arts.books" is a good starting point; there is also a newsgroup called "rec.arts.poems," and another devoted to "misc.writing." We should warn you that some of what we've seen posted on these newsgroups falls more into the realm of idle chitchat and doggerel than serious discussion, but we've found a number of worthwhile things, too: recently, some long and in-depth considerations of ideas about the line, and a number of lively responses to the question, "What is deconstructionism?" Newsgroups are a great way to connect with other writers, not only to share ideas and learn what people are thinking about, but also to get answers to practical questions, like finding the source of a particular quote or looking for good bookstores in a new city.

Many bookstores, literary journals, and audio archives are online as well. This means that you can order materials and subscribe to publications from home—often after previewing, or hearing, excerpts of the work. Looking for a particular article? A service called CARL will allow you to search for it and then download it for a fee. Want to stretch your knowledge with a writing or literature class? There are a number of them online, including one from The New School for Social Research, in New York City, which offers an electronic course in writing hypertext fiction and poetry. There are also live poetry readings happening in virtual "cafes," bringing together poets from all over.

We could go on and on—and still only scratch the surface. What we'd like to do is point you towards a few things we've found on the World Wide Web, and remind you that they are a microfraction of what's out there. Part of the fun is finding your own way from site to site, according to your needs or from plain curiosity, so take the plunge and use these references as jumping-off points for your own adventures.

On the Web, every journey starts with a single link; sites contain links to other sites, which link you to other sites, in an enormous, well, web of interconnected locations. We recommend starting with the search engine—an online database—at Stanford University known as Yahoo!. The address, or URL (Universal Resource Locator), is http://www.yahoo.com/Arts/Literature/Poetry/; from there you'll find a list of categories such as "Authors," "Awards," "Electronic Literature," "Literary E-Zines," "Poetry," "Theory," "Writing: Online Forums," and "Workshops." Additionally, if you click on "Indices," you'll find LitWeb, which lists newsgroups and other literary resources. There's also a book called the *Internet Yellow Pages* that lists online places of interest to writers, widely available at bookstores.

That's really all you need to know to get you going. But here's a list of a few sites we've come across that seem particularly worth visiting and will give you a sense of what's available. (A word of warning: As we said, things are changing fast; some of these URLs, current as of this writing, may have changed or disappeared by the time this book is in print.)

Literature:

The Academy of American Poets
http://www.tmn.com/Artswire/poets/page.html
This home page of the organization for writers offers a link to "Poetry on the Internet" where you can find the likes of Joseph Brodsky, E. E. Cummings, and T. S. Eliot.

Boson Books
http://www.cmonline.com
Books may be previewed online and then ordered via download or disk.

CAPA: The Contemporary American Poetry Archive
http://shain.lib.conncoll.edu/CAPA/capa.html
Directed by poet Wendy Battin, CAPA is "an electronic archive designed to make out-of-print volumes of poetry available to readers, scholars, and researchers."

Electronic Labyrinth
http://www.ualberta.ca/~ckeep/elab.html
An introduction to hyptertext for creative writers and artists: what it is, where it came from, some information about reading and writing it, works to read. You can learn about hypertext's development from postmodern theories and practices, and see where it's headed.

Electronic Library
http://www.books.com/scripts/lib.exe
Thousands of electronic books are available in a variety of subject areas, including the complete works of Shakespeare.

Electronic Poetry Center
http://wings.buffalo.edu/epc/presses
Small Press Page links to catalogs for Anvil Press, Burning Deck,

Meow Press, O Books, Roof Books, Station Hill, Story Line Press, and many others.

Emily Dickinson
http://lal.cs.byu.edu/people/black/dickinson.html
Here are 350 poems by Emily Dickinson, as well as links to everything you wanted to know, and more—from biographical information to audio recordings of her work, to her recipe for black cake!

English Server at CMU
http://english-server.hss.cmu.edu/
An archive with contemporary and classic works of fiction, drama, poetry, and criticism. Maya Angelou's famous inaugural poem, "On the Pulse of Morning," can be found here, along with Catullus, Coleridge, Ovid, Virgil, Sappho, Whitman, and more.

Hypertext Hotel
http://www.duke.edu/~mshumate/original.html
This is a collaborative fiction project which was begun by writer Robert Coover; it's another good place to start if you want to see what this new medium is all about. Coover first discussed hypertext and the project in an article which appeared in the *New York Times Book Review* in 1992. This site will link you to the article if you want to read it, along with other hypertext creations.

Internet Poetry Archive
http://sunsite.unc.edu/dykki/poetry/home.html
At this writing, the Archive is featuring work by Seamus Heaney and Czeslaw Milosz; you can see their photos, read and download their poems, and hear them as well.

Project Bartleby
http://www.cc.columbia.edu/acis/bartleby
"The Public Library of the Internet" has several hundred poems by Emily Dickinson, as well as works by Keats, Shelley, Whitman, the complete works of Wordsworth, and others.

Spectrum Press
http://users.aol.com/specpress/index.htm
Books on disk.

Voyager Books
http://www.voyagerco.com
A source for electronic books and CD-ROMs.

Walt Whitman Home Page
http://rs6.loc.gov/wwhome.html
Page by page, link by link, you can read, in his handwriting, the notebooks of Walt Whitman from the Thomas Biggs Harned collection. It's the next best thing to being there. A definite must for inspiration.

Literary Journals:
   There are over five hundred—and counting—journals currently on the Web. The work in these journals ranges from downright awful to truly wonderful. Some, such as the experimental journal *Avec*, the erotic journals *Libido* and *Yellow Silk*, and the *Paris Review*—are print publications which offer a selection of their contents online; others are true e-zines and exist only in cyberspace. Here are some sites we recommend:

Arts on the Net: Poets
http://www.art.net/poets.html
An attractively presented compilation of newer poets' work, including their photos.

The Atlantic Monthly
http://www2.theAtlantic.com/atlantic/
This is a popular site due to its "Poetry Pages" in the "Atlantic Unbound" link; you can find poets like Jane Hirshfield, Jane Kenyon, W. S. Merwin, and Robert Pinsky.

Grist On-line
http://www.thing.net/~grist/golpub/homegolp.htm
Tends toward experimental poetry. Anthologies like *Poets On the Line*; other e-zines.

Literal Latte
http://www.literal-latte.com
A Web version of the print journal distributed to cafes all over New York City. Has established a national presence. Small Press Review called it "one of the best new venues for any serious writer."

Mississippi Review Web
http://sushi.st.usm.edu/~barthelm/
A beautiful online monthly magazine, featuring fiction, poetry, essays, commentary, and reviews, published by the Center For Writers, the creative writing program at the University of Southern Mississippi. There's also a print edition. *Mississippi Review Web* has published work by such established poets as Margaret Atwood and Rita Dove, as well as newer writers.

Missouri Review
http://www.missouri.edu/~moreview/
Selected poets from past issues include Linda Hogan, Bin Ramke, and others.

Ploughshares
http://www.emerson.edu/ploughshares
This Web site contains a selection of work from the highly acclaimed print journal published at Emerson College in Boston.

Postmodern Culture
http://jefferson.village.virginia.edu/pmc/contents.all.html
"An Electronic Journal of Interdisciplinary Criticism" with a link called "PMC Fiction and Poetry."

Prism International
http://edziza.arts.ubc.ca/crwr/prism/prism.html
The established Canadian journal now has an online edition, and pays for both print and electronic publication.

Recursive Angel
http://www.calldei.com/~recangel/
Experimental poetry, fiction, and art. There's an annual print anthology from the best online work.

Silence
http://www.altx.com/silence/
This has been touted as the hot e-zine for the twentysomething crowd. A good place for the emerging writer.

Switched-on Gutenberg
http://weber.u.washington.edu/~jnh/
Edited by poet Jana Harris and billed as a "global poetry journal," the first issue went online in June 1995 and contains poems by Jane Hirshfield, Galway Kinnell, Edward Field, Joyce Carol Oates, and many others.

Sycamore Review
http://www.sla.purdue.edu/academic/engl/sycamore/
This journal from Purdue publishes entire out-of-print back issues online.

Third Coast
http://www.wmich.edu/thirdcoast/index.html
A selection of poetry and fiction from the journal published at Western Michigan University. Poets include Denise Duhamel, Richard Jackson, and Dean Young.

Web del Sol
http://www.cais.net/aesir/fiction
Experimental, literary, international, and mainstream poetry and fiction.

ZIPZAP
http://www.dnai.com/~zipzap/
Check out artists in the gallery, along with fiction, poetry, and interviews; links to *Deep Style* magazine and many other sites.

Spoken Word:

It's ironic that new technology enables poetry to return to its roots in the oral tradition; "Beowulf" was most likely sung to small groups, and the poet performed it to the accompaniment of a stringed instrument. Performance poetry, the widely popular medium for young

poets, is hardly new. The *Odyssey* was likely transferred down
through generations of listeners before Homer committed it to paper.
On the Web you can read a poem and hear (and see) the poet recit-
ing it, and perhaps discussing his approach to poetry and the particular poem as well. In that sense, you can be brought closer to the soul
of the work, and to the poet behind it. Just don't let it keep you from
going out to hear live poets; sitting at your computer can't equal the
energy and magic of a live reading, shared with an audience. To
appreciate these sites—and to actually listen to any of the writers on
the Web—you'll need to have a sound card for your computer.

Best-Quality Audio Web Poetry
http://www.cs.brown.edu:80/fun/bawp/

Electronic Poetry Center Sound Room
http://wings.buffalo.edu/epc/display/sound.html

Enterzone E-Zine
http://enterzone.berkeley.edu/ez/e2/sounds.html

The Green Island Spoken Audio Cooperative Library
http://www.crocker.com/%7Egisland/index.html
Audiobooks, lectures, readings, interviews, performances, and
other spoken word productions.

HarperCollins On-Line Audio Poetry
http://town.hall.org/Archives/radio/IMS/HarperAudio/
Samplings of audiobooks published by HarperCollins.

Workshops/Feedback:
Individual Manuscript Consultation
http://www.sonic.net/~scotts
Scott Reid, a Bay Area writer who generously shared some information and thoughts with us for this chapter, offers critiques
through his Web home page.

Online Writers Club
http://mhdstore2.moorhead.msus.edu/write/index.html

Riverview Writers Workshop
http://www.avalon.net/~jlinnell/rvw.html
Hosted by a group of University of Iowa students for feedback on poetry and fiction.

Straycat Writers Workshop
http://www.generation.net/~straycat/workshop.html
A place for writers to post poems or fiction for responses from other writers.

The Writers Gallery
http://www.writersg.com/writers/

Writers on the Net
http://www.writers.com/
There's a fee for this one.

As we've said, the above is a mere drop in the cyberbucket. But we hope it's enough to introduce you, however sketchily, to the astonishing array of literary offerings online. (Appendices C and D in this book list a few more online resources.) And we want to offer a caveat, as well. It's true that with computers, faxes, e-mail, the Internet, and the Web, communicating about writing is faster and easier. You can instantly get your work out to an editor or a friend, and just as quickly receive a response (though your friend is likely to get back to you sooner than an editor). Journals and presses are beginning to ask for submissions on disk, and if a journal is on a tight publishing schedule, you may be asked to fax or e-mail corrections or a biographical note once your work is accepted. With the Internet, you can have access to a world of ideas and information that is beyond anything previously possible—and there's much more to come. But reading and writing—hypertext aside—are still basically solitary activities, one-on-one experiences with reading someone else's language, or engaging with the deep place in your own psyche from which true poetry comes. The contemplative space, far from the noise of discussion and theory and video images, is not likely to be found online, but when the modem and telephone are turned off so you can create without distractions. Whether they carry a laptop or a spiral note-book, poets usually need to get away from others—even if it's only closing a door—in order to do their work. So by all means, enjoy what the electronic age has to offer in terms of convenience, ease, connection; but don't spend so much time netsurfing that you neglect the true work of a poet—simply to write.

Getting Published

Tell someone you're a writer, and nine out of ten times the response will be, "Are you published?" Imagine a surgeon being asked if she has ever operated on anyone, or a carpenter getting a raised eyebrow and a skeptical, "Ever built anything?" Still, it's no surprise that people expect serious writers to have published; and there's nothing like publication to make you feel like a Real Writer. Your work has spoken to someone; you have an audience, however small (many literary magazines have a circulation of only a few hundred copies); you have a real sense of validation for your efforts. All of these things can keep you going through the lonely hours of creating poems. And the anticipation of having your work read by an editor can help you take a good hard look at it, to push to make it that much better before you send it out.

But there's a downside to the whole business of submitting your work for publication. More often than not—and we mean *more often than not*—the poetry your friends praised and your workshop found "powerful," that you secretly felt was the best thing you'd ever done, gets returned in the mail. Rejected. The accompanying note may range from encouraging to downright chilly, but there it is: your work was turned down. Depending on the strength of your ego and what else is going on in your life, you may have a range of responses. You could laugh it off, marvel at the editor's appalling blindness to literary genius, and submit to the next journal on your list. Or you could feel bitter rage, followed by the urge to kidnap said editor's loved ones and hold them hostage until an entire issue of the journal is devoted to your work. Worse yet, you might simply feel completely worthless as a human being. One poet we know steels herself with a shot of scotch before opening any self-addressed stamped envelopes. There's no way to avoid rejection; it's a fact of life for every writer. You are, simply, never guaranteed publication, however good your work is, however many prizes and awards you may have collected along the way. And if you're just beginning to send your work out into the world, the indifference of that world—whether actual or only imagined—can be daunting.

So it's important that you are ready for the possibility of rejection before you begin the process. If you don't think you can take it, wait. If you recognize that you're a relative beginner, and haven't done your homework—that is, reading widely, studying, getting feedback on your work, revising until you feel the poems are polished—wait. Most people are in too much of a hurry. Writing poetry isn't about dashing off something inspired and dropping it in the mail; it's a process that requires a lot of work and care, and eventually, if you've made something worthwhile, you'll probably have the pleasure of passing it on in print, or in cyberspace. This doesn't mean you might not have some immediate success; in fact, with the wealth of journals geared to every taste, you have an excellent chance of getting published *somewhere*. If you want to publish just for the sake of publishing, that's relatively easy to do. We hope, though, that you'll see publication, not as an end in itself, but as icing on the cake—something to celebrate when it happens, but not the be-all and end-all of what writing is about.

Here are the questions people ask us most frequently:

Where should I submit my work?

There are a number of ways to find markets for your poems. Browse your local library or literary bookstore to see what journals they carry. Start with those published in your area; buy them, read them, and try to imagine your work within their pages. If possible, support a journal or two with a subscription; virtually all of them are struggling financially. You might find that certain journals prefer more experimental work; that others focus on special themes from issue to issue; that still others rarely publish new writers. A little such research can keep you from wasting time and postage sending out work that's likely to be returned.

Several good reference books that list markets for poets are widely available. We've listed them in Appendix C: "Finding Markets for Your Poems," along with some other sources. Also, national and local writers' organizations often put out newsletters which include calls for poetry submissions; you might want to consider joining one, or getting on their mailing list. Many online journals also accept e-mail and disk submissions; look under "Literary E-Zines" and "Poetry: Journals" listed by Yahoo!, the Stanford site whose address is given in the previous chapter.

You should also talk to your fellow writers and trade information. Teachers actively involved in the literary world may be able to recommend journals. If you find a published writer whose work seems similar to yours, look at the acknowledgments page of the book to see where the poems first appeared. Or pick up an anthology like the yearly *Pushcart Prize*, which lists participating magazines and presses with their addresses in the back.

How many poems should I send?

We suggest from three to six pages. Poems should always be typed or word-processed, one poem to a page. Put your name and address on each page; you'll quickly find that a pre-inked stamp comes in handy. Always include an SASE—sell-addressed stamped envelope—with sufficient postage for return of your work. If you don't want your work returned, simply say "SASE for reply only," and you'll only receive notification. Don't fold and refold the same poems several times and keep sending them out; better to copy fresh ones.

What about cover letters?

People seem to think cover letters are a big deal. In fact, some poets don't even bother with them. If you do include one, make sure it is brief and to the point. Ask the editor to consider your work; if you've published previously, mention where your poetry has appeared. You could add a line about yourself—"I'm a graduate student at Berkeley," or "I have eleven children and an unfortunate history of madness," or "I've just received the Pulitzer." If you have read the journal and enjoyed a particular piece, by all means say so. Editors like to know their hard work is appreciated. Don't send a lengthy list of publications, or a long biographical sketch, or a delineation of the major themes of your poetry and its sources.

How do editors feel about simultaneous submissions?

This is a tricky one. The general rule is: Don't send your work to more than one magazine at a time. Although this policy has changed somewhat, the majority of journals don't like to consider and accept a piece, then find out it has been taken elsewhere. The downside is that some journals take so long to respond that your work might only get seen by one or two a year *unless* you send it out to two—or more—places at once. Given the competitive nature of the process, the odds are against you, and you can increase them with simultaneous submissions. But if the same poem gets taken by two journals, you're going to be in a sticky situation. *Poet's Market* lists the journals that do consider simultaneous submissions. There was a good discussion of this topic in the September/October 1992 issue of *Poets & Writers*; check it out at the library, or write Poets & Writers for a back issue.

How long do I wait for a response to my submission?

Sometimes forever. We are not kidding; some journals seem particularly adept at losing poems. Then there are those which fold because of lack of funds, or because the editor's husband ran off with the proofreader, or for any number of reasons. The average length of time to wait is about three months. After that, write a note and enclose another SASE, asking when you might have a response. If you don't get a response or your poems returned in the mail within another month, you might send a note saying you'll be submitting elsewhere.

Should I submit again to a magazine that has rejected my work?

Sure; why not? If you've received something beyond a form rejection—a handwritten "Sorry," perhaps some mention of a poem that almost made it—you should definitely submit again. Something about your poetry stood out enough to attract interest. Most editors are underpaid (or unpaid), overworked, and swamped with submissions. They have to rely on form rejections, and can rarely offer critiques. So be assured that if you've received a more personal response, the editor is receptive to your work. (There are a few exceptions, but they're rare.) Even a form rejection doesn't indicate that your work won't meet with favor the next time. The reasons for rejection are many, and don't always have to do with the quality of the work. An editor may have seen fifty poems about death that day, and so decide on something more uplifting than the elegy you wrote. Be persistent, wherever and whenever there is a hint of interest.

What about copyrighting my work?

No one we know copyrights poems. There's a simple reason for this: Sad as it may seem, poems aren't marketable. No Hollywood agent is going to swoop down to steal your sonnet sequence, make it into a major motion picture, and abscond with the profits. If you're still concerned, you should know that according to U.S. copyright laws, your work is protected as soon as you write it; creating it makes you the copyright owner. You can, if you have money to burn, write to the U.S. Copyright Office and pay to register your poems. We think there are better ways to use that kind of discretionary income—like subscribing to literary journals. Don't, under any circumstances, put a little copyright symbol on your poetry thinking this will make you appear a professional; in fact, just the opposite is true. You should know that most journals, when they agree to publish your work, want what is called "first publication rights"; that is, they want the exclusive right to publish the poem before any other journal. When the magazine appears, such rights automatically revert to the author. If you still want to learn more about copyright registration, write the U.S. Copyright Office, Library of Congress, Washington, DC 20559.

How do writers keep track of submissions?

You should always keep a record not only of where you send your poems, but the date of submission and the date you receive an answer. If you send to the same journal more than once, you can check your records to see how long it generally takes for that particular journal to respond; and you'll avoid sending the same poems to a place that has already turned them down. If an editor praises a specific poem even though declining, you might have a clue about what work to send next time. Some people prefer to keep records on their computers; others rely on a spiral notebook and paste in responses from editors; still others file information on index cards. It's helpful to know where you're going to make the next submission, so you can keep your work circulating.

What about self-publishing?

Some writers put together collections of their poetry for friends and family; others, frustrated by rejections, may seek other means of getting their work before the world. Still others start their own presses to produce their work and that of poets they admire. Many writers, including Walt Whitman, self-published; and with desktop printing, you don't need to pay a typesetter anymore. But if you want to go this route, remember that printing is not the same as publishing. Your chapbook or book, no matter how beautifully produced, is going to sit in boxes in the closet unless you can find a distributor. Chapbooks—those small, staple-bound collections—do not generally find their way to bookstores and distributors; they must be displayed face-front and take up too much shelf space. And even with a perfect-bound book, it is difficult to convince a distributor of reasonable sales unless you have a track record in recognized literary journals. If you're printing up copies to sell at readings, and possibly to convince a local bookstore owner to carry your work, great. If you're looking for a wider audience, be prepared to put a lot of time and energy into creating your own press. There *are* some distributors who are sympathetic to small, independent efforts; one is Small Press Distribution in Berkeley. You can find a list of distributors in *The International Directory of Little Magazines and Small Presses* from Dustbooks; the address is listed in Appendix D, "More Resources for Writers." Another possibility—and one that neatly solves the distribution problem—is to start your own home page on the World Wide Web, and "publish" your poems in cyberspace. Though you won't have a hard copy, you will at least have readers—and they can respond to your work directly. (See Appendix D, "More Resources for Writers," for information on starting your own Web page.)

What can I expect from publication?

Strangers will stop you on the street for your autograph. You will no longer have to wait in line at the post office or be cut off by rude drivers. Parents, friends, and neighbors will gaze at you with respect and envy. Your sex life will improve dramatically. You will never feel lonely again.

Okay, so we're kidding. Secretly, though, many of us expect that publishing will somehow magically transform our lives. It can be deflating, after the initial euphoria of acceptance, to wait several months to over a year to see your work published, then receive your one or two contributor's copies in the mail (and sometimes a very small check) and realize that nothing's changed. You're still struggling with your writing; since that acceptance, ten journals have turned you down; no limousine has appeared at your door to whisk you off to a star-studded publication party.

In fact, wonderful things can, and do, result from publishing. But these things, for the most part, happen slowly, and are less dramatic than you might hope. An editor, once introduced to your work, might ask to see more. An appreciative reader might write you a fan letter; you'll know you've reached someone with your words. If you've published in a local journal, there may be a publication party, at which you can read for an audience and meet other writers. The two authors of this book met at such a party over ten years ago. Publishing puts your poetry in front of strangers who may become your friends and colleagues, but who are in any case your readers; whether you meet them in person or not, you've shared an intimate exchange on the page.

TWENTY-MINUTE
WRITING EXERCISES

Can you write a poem in twenty minutes? We seriously doubt it. What you can do, though, is get one started; having a time limit can keep you focused on the task at hand and help you push past the urge to get up from your desk and clean out the cat box or call your best friend.

The rules for these exercises are simple. First, read the assignment and the model poem, if there is one. When you've done that, set the timer for twenty minutes. Try to keep writing the entire time; try to stick with the instructions, but if you don't, that's fine. The idea is to trigger a poem, not to see how well you follow directions. Don't worry if what comes out is messy, shapeless, or weird; that's exactly what *should* come out in a first draft. Later, you can go back to the raw material generated by the exercise and work on it. We recommend doing these exercises when you're feeling blocked, or when time is at a premium, or when you get together with other people to write.

A Simple Exercise

This was an exercise given to a class of advanced students. The rules were simple:

1. Write about writing. All of us, at some time or other, are tempted to write an *ars poetica*. Most such poems don't work out. It's as if we are too close to our subject matter; we tend to get maudlin and sentimental about what we love. It's a difficult task and you will probably fail. But when has that ever stopped us? Go ahead. Write about writing.

2. It's cold outside.

3. It should be snowing by now, but isn't.

4. Identify the time of day.

5. Use the pronoun "we." Our culture is enamored of the concept of "the individual," and because of this much of our writing employs the use of the lyric "I." It's very American, very "twentieth century," and sets us apart from poets of other cultures, who tend to be more inclusive, connected to each other by circumstance, politics, poverty, or simple population density. It's an interesting exercise to try to think as a group, to speak as a group, for others as well as for yourself. There's a wonderful novel by Joan Chase called *During the Reign of the Queen of Sheba* in which the narrator speaks as a group of sisters.

Siblings have that special feeling of connection and shared experience, as do families in general, as well as close friends and lovers. Try for this feeling when you use the word "we."

6. Use the word "florid" in a way it would not be normally used. (Or any other word you choose. Close your eyes and scan a dictionary or newspaper with your finger. Stop. Use that word. Or ask a friend to choose a word for you. Use a word you've always loved and wanted to get into a poem. Be sure to use your word in an original or nontraditional way.)

Here's a student poem that came out of this exercise:

BARE BRANCHES

> *"What would they say if they knew*
> *I sit for two months on six lines*
> *of poetry?"*
>
> —Lorine Niedecker

This stark room, how simple, they say,
they not being we
who know it's easy to be florid,
not get
to the gut.

The bare branches of the maple satisfy me.
Maybe by noon a bird will perch on one
like a word on a blank page.
Soon, I hope, the snow will come,
complete the landscape.

The snow is miraculous every time it arrives,
like a poem.

—Stephanie Mendel

What's wonderful about this poem is that it asks us to be patient as writers, tells us that poems don't come often or easily. And yet this poet didn't simply sit around waiting for a poem to appear before her, free of charge; she worked at doing exercises in an effort to get the poem to come to her. This is one of the joys of exercises; you can do them while you're waiting for a poem to appear, and if you're lucky, and work hard, maybe a poem will indeed appear. Obviously this poet had been thinking about that quote by Niedecker for some time. Maybe she wanted to say something about it but couldn't. Maybe she didn't even know she wanted to say something about it, but the exercise sparked her imagination. Not every exercise will work for you; in fact, most exercises fail as fully realized poems. But even if you can get one good stanza to work with, a good line, even a new word or a title to add to your storehouse, the exercise has been worth the time it took to do it.

In a U-Haul North of Damascus

Paul, formerly Saul, of biblical fame, experienced his great conversion on the road to Damascus. He was traveling there to speak against Jesus and when Jesus appeared to him on the road and blinded him he became a believer. David Bottoms has taken the story of a man who has sinned and is on his way to conversion and made it a moving contemporary story about divorce. Using the Bottoms poem as a model, write a poem about driving to or from a place you either love or hate. Mention at least two road signs—SLOW, STOP, MERGE, Sausalito Exit 2 Miles, etc. . . . and one establishment—a cafe, a hotel, a gas station, etc. Try to see these signs as SIGNS, the establishments as SYMBOLIC. The poem must include a list of concrete objects. Somewhere in the poem you might try recounting either your sins or failures. Begin or end the poem with a question.

1

Lord, what are the sins
I have tried to leave behind me? The bad checks,
the workless days, the scotch bottles thrown across the fence
and into the woods, the cruelty of silence,
the cruelty of lies, the jealousy,
the indifference?

What are these on the scale of sin
or failure
that they should follow me through the streets of Columbus,
the moon-streaked fields between Benevolence
and Cuthbert where dwarfed cotton sparkles like pearls
on the shoulders of the road. What are these
that they should find me half-lost,
sick and sleepless
behind the wheel of this U-Haul truck parked in a field on Georgia
45
a few miles north of Damascus,
some makeshift rest stop for eighteen wheelers
where the long white arms of oaks slap across trailers
and headlights glare all night through a wall of pines?

2

What was I thinking, Lord?
That for once I'd be in the driver's seat, a firm grip
on direction?

So the jon boat muscled up the ramp,
the Johnson outboard, the bent frame of the wrecked Harley
chained for so long to the back fence,
the scarred desk, the bookcases and books,
the mattress and box springs,
a broken turntable, a Pioneer amp, a pair
of three-way speakers, everything mine
I intended to keep. Everything else abandon.

But on the road from one state
to another, what is left behind nags back through the distance,
a last word rising to a scream, a salad bowl
shattering against a kitchen cabinet, china barbs
spiking my heel, blood trailed across the cream linoleum
like the bedsheet that morning long ago
just before I watched the future miscarried.

Jesus, could the irony be
that suffering forms a stronger bond than love?

3

Now the sun
streaks the windshield with yellow and orange, heavy beads
of light drawing highways in the dew-cover.
I roll down the window and breathe the pine-air,
the after-scent of rain, and the far-off smell
of asphalt and diesel fumes.

But mostly pine and rain
as though the world really could be clean again.

Somewhere behind me,
miles behind me on a two-lane that streaks across
west Georgia, light is falling
through the windows of my half-empty house.
Lord, why am I thinking about all this? And why should I care
so long after everything has fallen
to pain that the woman sleeping there should be sleeping alone?
Could I be just another sinner who needs to be blinded
before he can see? Lord, is it possible to fall
toward grace? Could I be moved
to believe in new beginnings? Could I be moved?

The Language of the Brag

I have wanted excellence in the knife-throw,
I have wanted to use my exceptionally strong and accurate arms
and my straight posture and quick electric muscles
to achieve something at the center of a crowd,
the blade piercing the bark deep,
the haft slowly and heavily vibrating like the cock.

I have wanted some epic use for my excellent body,
some heroism, some American achievement
beyond the ordinary for my extraordinary self,
magnetic and tensile, I have stood by the sandlot
and watched the boys play.

I have wanted courage, I have thought about fire
and the crossing of waterfalls, I have dragged around

my belly big with cowardice and safety,
my stool black with iron pills,
my huge breasts oozing mucus,
my legs swelling, my hands swelling,
my face swelling and darkening, my hair
falling out, my inner sex
stabbed again and again with terrible pain like a knife.
I have lain down.

I have lain down and sweated and shaken
and passed blood and feces and water and

slowly alone in the center of a circle I have
passed the new person out
and they have lifted the new person free of the act
and wiped the new person free of that
language of blood like praise all over the body.

I have done what you wanted to do, Walt Whitman,
Allen Ginsberg, I have done this thing,
I and the other women this exceptional
act with the exceptional heroic body,
this giving birth, this glistening verb,
and I am putting my proud American boast
right here with the others.

—Sharon Olds

Write a brag poem. Brainstorm a list of things you're good at, moments in your life when you achieved perfection, or something close to it. We sometimes tend to be afraid of bringing attention to ourselves and our accomplishments. What have you done that you're proud of? Why should others envy you? Choose one item from your list and expand on it, or use the whole list! Apply large words to yourself: courageous, glorious, excellence, power, brilliance. Write as if you are applying for a job as the perfect human being, or be more specific—the perfect friend, mother, child, wife, son, sister, lover, gardener, bus driver, cook, tax consultant, political activist, doctor, warden, president, thief, anything you were, are, or want to be. Boast!

Beauty

Death is the mother of beauty.
—Wallace Stevens, "Sunday Morning"

Beauty is as beauty does.
—Proverb

"Beauty is truth, truth beauty,"—that is all
Ye know on earth, and all ye need to know.
—John Keats, "Ode on a Grecian Urn"

The beautiful is the unusual.
—?

Beauty is in the eye of the beholder.
—Proverb

Beauty fades.
—character in the film "Desperately Seeking Susan,"
speaking of Susan, played by Madonna

Using one of these ideas as a starting point, write a poem that either
argues or agrees with it. Describe *one* beautiful thing, *in detail*, in the
poem. Avoid conventional, stereotypical images—sunsets, laughing
children, fields of flowers. Instead, look for something a bit unex-

pected, and describe it so we see and understand its beauty. The trick here is to make your argument or agreement—that is, your point about beauty—through your imagery. You may want to make a statement or two as well, but try to avoid sounding rhetorical or preachy.

Do You Want a Chicken Sandwich

What's your most acutely embarrassing moment? We wonder if you can top this one, described by Norman Stock in his bizarrely wonderful book, *Buying Breakfast for my Kamikaze Pilot.*

> the time my mother opened the door
> to the living room and saw me on my knees
> with my hard cock in my hand jerking off
> in front of the television set with a hot magazine at my side
> and she gasped and quickly shut the door
> but she did finish what she started to say
> when she first pushed it open which was
> do you want a chicken sandwich
> okay I probably said to the door and put my cock back in my pants
> and went and ate my chicken sandwich
> while in the next room through all of this embarrassment
> my father was playing the violin always the same old song

Write a poem describing, in excruciating detail, a moment of embarrassment. Such incidents are often funny—after the fact, of course. Try to see, and convey, the humor in your situation.

American Burying Beetle

For this exercise you'll first need to do a bit of research. Pick an animal that intrigues you, or even one that repels you. Find out how it lives, mates, eats, etc. You might get your information from a book on animals, the encyclopedia, a nature show on television, or the science pages of the newspaper. Make some notes, and be sure to include interesting words specifically related to that animal. Once you've done that, you're ready to sit down and write, to let your imagination work on the raw facts and transform them into something poetic. This poem by Barbara Helfgott Hyett is from *The Tracks We Leave*, a book of poems about endangered wildlife.

> They kill nothing, but fly to the site
> at the slightest whiff of the just-dead—
> one small body slipping toward
> eternity, each cell giving in, the corpse
> of an unfledged finch sinking inexorably,
> a fraction of an inch at a time.
>
> Beneath the carcass, a beetle pair,
> on their backs, digging, twelve legs
> thrust as levers, four claws shoveling
> earth away. The grave fills with a body
> turning to rankness, form transforming.

Beetles depend on the opening death
brings. They pull out every feather,
make flesh ripen into green.

On the altar of existence they condense
life to liquefaction. And when their larvae
waken, white and blind, they will press
palps upon them, one after another,
let them sip from that pool. Flags unfurl
from the tips of their antennae; black
bellies rasp against the crimson scarves
of wings. These are the sorcerer's markings:
death diminished, pulled out from under, undone.

For the Sleepwalkers

Tonight I want to say something wonderful
for the sleepwalkers who have so much faith
in their legs, so much faith in the invisible

arrow carved into the carpet, the worn path
that leads to the stairs instead of the window,
the gaping doorway instead of the seamless mirror.

I love the way that sleepwalkers are willing
to step out of their bodies into the night,
to raise their arms and welcome the darkness,

palming the blank spaces, touching everything.
Always they return home safely, like blind men
who know it is morning by feeling shadows.

And always they wake up as themselves again.
That's why I want to say something astonishing
like: *Our hearts are leaving our bodies.*

*Our hearts are thirsty black handkerchiefs
flying through the trees at night, soaking up
the darkest beams of moonlight, the music*

*of owls, the motion of wind-torn branches.
And now our hearts are thick black fists
flying back to the glove of our chests.*

We have to learn to trust our hearts like that.
We have to learn the desperate faith of sleepwalkers who rise out of their calm beds

and walk through the skin of another life.
We have to drink the stupefying cup of darkness
and wake up to ourselves, nourished and surprised.

—Edward Hirsch

Write a poem of praise for an unlikely group of people, things, ideas—whatever or whoever you think has gotten short shrift or a bad rap. Do as Hirsch does and about halfway through the poem insert a colon and then leap off and dare to say something overtly beautiful or poetic, bizarre or funny. Then return to the poem and tell us what this group has to teach us about ourselves. Also notice how Hirsch uses the letter "w" throughout his poem and how, like a thread, it helps to pull us through the poem. Choose a letter and try weaving it into the language, but don't be overly alliterative—be subtle.

I Believe

Few of us really know what we believe until we're pressed into thinking about it. As poets, we must know what our boundaries are, even if only to break though them. If we expect to be believed, we need to know what we believe and then question, without mercy, those very beliefs.

In the movie "Bull Durham," Kevin Costner plays a baseball player named Crash Davis; Susan Sarandon is a woman named Annie. Consider this exchange:

Crash: I don't believe in quantum physics when it comes to matters of the heart.
Annie: What do you believe in, then?
Crash: I believe in the soul, the cock, the pussy, the small of a woman's back, the hanging curve ball, high fiber, good scotch, that the novels of Susan Sontag are self-indulgent, overrated crap. I believe Lee Harvey Oswald acted alone; I believe there ought to be a congressional amendment outlawing astroturf and the designated hitter; I believe in the sweet spot, softcore pornography, opening your presents Christmas morning rather than Christmas Eve; and I believe in long, slow, deep, soft, wet kisses that last three days.

In the novel *Crooked Hearts* by Robert Boswell, a character named Ask has a list of rules he carries in his wallet. These are his rules:

1. Never make a complicated thing simple, or a simple thing complicated.
2. Wear white at night.
3. Take care of Tom. [Ask's brother.]
4. Eat from the four food groups.
5. Be consistent.
6. Never do anything with the sole intent of hurting someone.
7. Floss.
8. Always put the family first.
9. Clean even where it doesn't show.
10. Pursue the truth.
11. Wear socks that match your shirt.
12. Take care of Cassie. [Ask's sister.]
13. Look up words you don't know.
14. Never put out electrical flames with water.
15. Get to the bottom of things.
16. If a person changes his or her hair, tell him or her it looks good.
17. Remember.
18. Forgive.

Then there's Maria in Joan Didion's novel, *Play It As It Lays*:

She would never: walk through the Sands or Caesar's alone after midnight. She would never: ball at a party, do S-M unless she wanted to, borrow furs from Abe Lipsey, deal. She would never: carry a Yorkshire in Beverly Hills.

And finally, here's a short poem by Steve Kowit:

CREDO

I am of those who believe
different things on different days.

Okay; now you are ready for the exercise. Build an authoritative voice; write an "I Believe" speech. Brainstorm a list of six things you seriously believe in, and another list of three silly or outrageous beliefs. Make another list of six rules for yourself: four as a person and two as a poet. Then add two statements of disbelief and three statements of things you would never do. Stir them all together and see what happens.

Asking for Directions

We could have been mistaken for a married couple
riding on the train from Manhattan to Chicago
that last time we were together. I remember
looking out the window and praising the beauty
of the ordinary: the in-between places, the world
with its back turned to us, the small neglected
stations of our history. I slept across your
chest and stomach without asking permission
because they were the last hours. There was
a smell to the sheepskin lining of your new
Chinese vest that I didn't recognize. I felt
it deliberately. I woke early and asked you
to come with me for coffee. You said, sleep more,
and I said we only had one hour and you came.
We didn't say much after that. In the station,
you took your things and handed me the vest,
then left as we had planned. So you would have
ten minutes to meet your family and leave.
I stood by the seat dazed by exhaustion
and the absoluteness of the end, so still I was
aware of myself breathing. I put on the vest
and my coat, got my bag and, turning, saw you
through the dirty window standing outside looking
up at me. We looked at each other without any

expression at all. Invisible, unnoticed, still.
That moment is what I will tell of as proof
that you loved me permanently. After that I was
a woman alone carrying her bag, asking a worker
which direction to walk to find a taxi.

                                  —Linda Gregg

Write a poem about the last time you saw a loved one you lost. Address the poem to that person. Include an abstract statement about the relationship. End the poem with something that you did alone, afterwards, an ordinary gesture or action that embodies the emotions you felt.

Anniversary

Write about what you were doing this time last year, or the year before; what anniversaries would you mark? Don't think just in terms of a death, or meeting someone, or an illness, or a holiday observance—though these are all possibilities. Think about what your life was like in this season, in this month.

Use five of the following words: swan, root, mask, pleasure, blind, believe, sit, curtain, flames, love.

Use a proper name in the poem.

Combine something in the present with that past memory.

Talking to God

This poem was written by Susan Browne, who teaches poetry at Diablo Valley College in California. She also attended our workshops, as well as various writers' conferences, to gain inspiration and ideas for her own poetry. Susan proves that the work of learning never ends. Here's her poem:

POEM IN MY MOTHER'S VOICE

When my mother meets God,
she says, *Where the hell have you been?*
Jesus Christ, don't you care about anyone
but yourself? It's time you wake up,
smell the coffee, shit or get off the pot.

You must have won your license in a fucking raffle.
You're grounded, and I don't want any back-talk.
In fact, don't talk at all until you can say something
that is not a lie, until you can tell the truth.
You know, the truth? Something in sentence form
that comes out of your mouth and is not a lie.
Could you do that for me? Is this possible
in my lifetime? Don't ever lie to me again
or I'll kill you. And get off your high-horse,
WHO DO YOU THINK YOU ARE?

Running around the world
like a goddamn maniac, creating havoc. You have lost
the good sense you were born with. Shape up or ship out.
I can't believe we're related.

My mother lights a cigarette, pitches the match
through the strings of a harp, inhales profoundly,
letting the smoke billow from her nose.
Her ruby lips press together in a righteous grimace
of disgust. She never stops watching God.

I've really had enough this time.
What do you take me for? A fool? An idiot? A patsy?
Some kind of nothing set down on earth for your convenience,
entertainment? A human punching bag? For your information,
I was not born yesterday. I know what you're up to.
I have been around the block a few thousand spins of the wheel.
I have more compassion in my little finger
than you have in your entire body. I am a mother.
I care. Maybe you don't care, but I do. Care.
Do you know what that word means? Bring me the dictionary
and I will tell you what the word care means. Never mind.
How could you find a dictionary in that dump you call a room.
The whole universe of care down the toilet
because of your dirty socks. Do I look like a maid?
Did you think the purpose of my existence was to serve you?
You are barking up the wrong tree. We need to get something
straight: I am not here for you. I am here for me.
But I care. Can you possibly, in your wildest imagination,
hold two ideas in your tiny mind at the same time?
This is called paradox. Par-a-dox. We need the dictionary.
No, we need to talk. What do you have to say for yourself?

"I'm sorry," God replies.

You're sorry. Well, that's not enough. Wash that sullen look
off your face, or I'll wash it off for you.
And quit looking down. Look at me!

God lifts his heavy head,
falls into the fierce love
of my mother's green-blue eyes.

Grow up, she says.

Write a poem to God. Make it a tirade, an outburst, a slanderous harangue. Let yourself go. Or, write a poem in God's voice; let God explain, refute, deny, defend. Make it a monologue or a conversation, whatever you like. Or let God be a traffic cop, a rock star, a porn queen, a manicurist. Notice how Browne's poem consists mostly of clichés and yet, because of the context she puts them in, they sound fresh, funny, new. Use at least one cliché in your poem, but make it new. For instance, musician Sheryl Crow sings "I'm standing in the desert, waiting for my ship to come in."

Star Dust

In a small history of the Great Plains
a band of Indians plunders a keelboat
stowing fortunes of gold dust
in buckskin sacks. Once the cargo
is theirs, they keep the durable,
the leather—for packing chokecherries
and buffalo—let the gold
mix with the sand, the element gimcrack,
star dust to the Sioux.
And pausing in my reading
I juxtapose romance
against these work-mastered days,
love's ticking metal, the sparkle-
mask of unworkable love, neither steady
nor enduring. Gleaming, luring.

                                    —Stefanie Marlis

Write a poem that begins with something you've read. Then, as
Marlis does, look up from the page and connect it to your life.

Revere Me

Here's a poem by Ruth Schwartz, whose manuscript *Accordion Breathing and Dancing* was chosen as the 1994 winner of the Associated Writing Programs first-book competition.

BATH

Through the hot water, your belly,
your lovely, fat, floating, abused belly,
flesh you stick with daily needles
which bruises, sometimes, into purple blossom.
Desire branches there teeth-first,
taking us both.
Love, to describe you
perhaps I should start with your feet,
scaly and nerveless, toenails gone,
flesh crusted-over in their place.
Under your skin the kidneys bloat, helpless to let go
the long, clean, clear streams of urine,
and when you walk a block, or up a flight of stairs,
your arteries choke shut and airless,
panting on their little tracks—
how far away it seems, that castle,
your struggling heart.

Sometimes you look to me like an old woman,
despairing and fat.
Still, your breasts float toward me,
hot, wet, buoyant moons
I can hold in my two hands,
and still, when we gather each other,
rolling and sliding into sudden, holy want,
the body says "Revere me,"
                                   and I do.

We were struck by this poem because it so graphically describes what might be ugly, and transforms that ugliness through love. The poet doesn't romanticize her loved one; she sees her clearly, wholly, and dares to portray a less-than-idealized image. Look hard at something, or someone, and write your own love poem; try to describe that object or person in all their glorious, messy, unpleasant, amazing aspects.

Suppose

Carl Dennis has a lovely poem about writing called "Useful Advice" in his book *A House of My Own*. Here's the exercise we devised, based on some aspects of his poem: begin with the word "Suppose," address the reader directly, and include something surreal or unlikely. Maureen Micus Crisick wrote the following:

SUPPOSE

the ghetto stars pinned to cloth
could lift from history
like angels soaring to the sky.
The air which holds cinders
of Buddhist robes, burned hair
of ones who doused themselves, set fire,
suppose the plume of smoke
becomes clear and white.

What did I say?
I said: what if Sarajevo is not burning
and no city is burning
and in the market square
no human head is impaled on a stick
or mute limbs strewn on streets,
and no fingers exist without hands.

Suppose grenades side with sunlight.
Bullets in boxes become
chocolate wrapped in gold foil,
and in Guatemala, the men come back
from their disappearance,
and in the morning, wake in their own beds
because love is the white moon
and light moves in us like blood.

Yes
there will be holes left in clothes
but not from ripped stars,
only from wear,
to let the darkness out.

Appendix A:
Books on Poetry and Writing

Behn, Robin and Twichell, Chase, eds. *The Practice of Poetry: Writing Exercises from Poets Who Teach.* HarperCollins, 1992. Here are a number of wonderful exercises sure to trigger new work, including some for groups—perfect for a class or a workshop. An added bonus is that a number of the poets who contributed the exercises talk a bit about what the exercise is designed to teach—from accessing the unconscious to a better grasp of metaphor, structure, etc.

Boisseau, Michelle and Wallace, Robert. *Writing Poems.* Fourth Edition. HarperCollins, 1996. A comprehensive text with wonderfully lucid discussions of how poems work, including many excellent poems for both analysis and inspiration.

Boland, Eavan. *Object Lessons: The Life of the Woman and the Poet in Our Time.* W. W. Norton, 1995. In eleven autobiographical essays, Boland explores how the tradition of womanhood and the historic vocation of the poet act as revealing illuminations of the other.

Chi, Lu. *Wen Fu (The Art of Writing).* Translated by Sam Hamill. Milkweed Editions, 1991. This little book, written in the third century, is the first *ars poetica* of China. The short, lyrical sections point toward enlightened living and writing.

Comley, Nancy; Scholes, Robert; and Ulmer, Gregory. *Text Book: An Introduction to Literary Language.* St. Martin's Press, 1988. A book which foregrounds literature as text, with many provocative ideas and exercises for a developing writer. There's a lot of good material on metaphor and how it structures both language and thinking, as well as suggestions for experimentation.

DesPres, Terrence. *Praises and Dispraises: Poetry and Politics, the 20th Century.* Penguin, 1988. A beautiful, passionate book about poets, and poems, in the world, focusing on a handful: Brecht, Breytenbach, McGrath, Rich, Yeats.

Drake, Barbara. *Writing Poetry.* Second Edition. Harcourt Brace & Company, 1994. A friendly and informative book that also has a generous selection of good writing exercises to get you going.

Friebert, Stuart and Young, David, eds. *A Field Guide to Contemporary Poetry and Poetics.* Longman, Inc., 1980. A variety of essays about poetry and poetic practice, including a "symposium on the line" with contributors like Donald Hall and Sandra McPherson.

Fussell, Paul. *Poetic Meter & Poetic Form.* Random House, 1965. In-depth discussions of prosody, with close analysis of many metered poems.

Gioia, Dana. *Can Poetry Matter?* Graywolf Press, 1992. The title essay of this book caused a big fuss when it was first published in the *Atlantic* in 1991, with its critical look at poetry as an isolated academic subculture. A critic and poet often associated with the new formalists, Gioia discusses that phenomenon, as well as a number of writers, including Wallace Stevens, Ted Kooser, John Ashbery, and Maxine Kumin.

Glück, Louise. *Proofs & Theories: Essays on Poetry.* The Ecco Press, 1994. The Pulitzer Prize-winning poet discusses the education of the poet, considers the notion of characterizing poetry as "courageous," and offers chapters titled "Against Sincerity," "The Forbidden," "The Dreamer and the Watcher," among others. Discussions of a number of poets and poetic strategies along the way.

Goldberg, Natalie. *Wild Mind: Living the Writer's Life.* Bantam Books, 1990. Goldberg is also the author of an earlier book on writing, *Writing Down the Bones: Freeing the Writer Within.* Both come from the author's experience as a Zen student, writer, and teacher, and offer encouragement and advice about the writing process.

Hass, Robert. *Twentieth Century Pleasures: Prose on Poetry.* The Ecco Press, 1984. The 1995–96 Poet Laureate of the United States offers informal essays on craft and process, discussing writers such as Lowell, Milosz, Rilke, and others.

Hirshfield, Jane. *Nine Gates: Entering the Mind of Poetry.* HarperCollins, 1997.

Hugo, Richard. *The Triggering Town: Lectures and Essays on Poetry and Writing.* W. W. Norton, 1992. This little book, whose dedication reads "For all students of creative writing—and for their teachers," has been read and enjoyed by both since its publication. Hugo writes interesting and engaging prose about craft, process, and practicalities.

Kowit, Steve. *In the Palm of Your Hand: The Poet's Portable Workshop.* Tilbury House, 1995. An accessible, thorough approach to writing with excellent step-by-step exercises that guide you toward finished poems, along with a good treatment of both traditional forms and experimental approaches.

Kuusisto, Stephen; Tall, Deborah; and Weiss, David, eds. *The Poet's Notebook: Excerpts from the Notebooks of Contemporary American Poets.* W. W. Norton, 1995. Includes excerpts from the working notebooks of twenty-six American poets.

Lamott, Anne. *Bird by Bird: Some Instructions on Writing and Life.* Pantheon, 1994. With frankness and wit, Lamott discusses the writing process and the writing life.

Mayes, Frances. *The Discovery of Poetry*. Second Edition. Harcourt Brace, 1994. A useful, informative, and highly readable textbook that includes a large selection of poems old and new, as well as advice on writing student essays about poetry, and a number of good, inspiring writing exercises.

McDowell, Robert, ed. *Poetry After Modernism*. Story Line Press, 1991. A collection of essays by various writers with the stated goal of "mak[ing] sense, finally, of modernism and its aftermath." Topics include "Poetry and Politics," "Poetry and Religion," "The Feminist Literary Movement," "Modern Afro-American Poetry," and others.

Nelson, Victoria. *On Writer's Block: A New Approach to Creativity*. Houghton Mifflin, 1993. A fascinating book on the creative process and on how our conscious and subconscious mind need to cooperate for the free flow of words. Whether or not you've ever felt stuck with your writing, you'll find much here that's of interest.

Olsen, Tillie. *Silences*. Delacorte Press, 1978. The author of *Tell Me a Riddle* explores the ways that creative work is thwarted, culling examples from her own life (she stopped writing for twenty years) and the lives of other writers, including selections from their diaries and journals.

Padgett, Ron, ed. *The Teachers & Writers Handbook of Poetic Forms*. Teachers & Writers Collaborative, 1987. Seventy-four entries on traditional and modern poetic forms by nineteen teaching writers.

Pinsky, Robert. *Poetry and the World*. The Ecco Press, 1988. Essays on poetry's place in the modern world. Pinsky combines the arts of criticism and autobiography to write about poets as diverse as Walt Whitman, Philip Freneau, Marianne Moore, and Frank O'Hara.

Pinsky, Robert. *The Situation of Poetry: Contemporary Poetry and Its Traditions*. Princeton University Press, 1976. An invigorating look at twentieth century poetic tradition, as well as a look back to Keats's "Ode to a Nightingale" and what Pinsky calls "The Romantic Persistence" in modern and contemporary writing. Lucid discussions of Robert Lowell, John Berryman, Wallace Stevens, Louise Bogan, John O'Hara, A. R. Ammons, and others.

Preminger, Alex, ed. *New Princeton Encyclopedia of Poetry and Poetics*. Princeton University Press, 1993. Curious about Slavic prosody? About the origins of the pastoral or the history of narrative poetry? Want to refresh your memory about T. S. Eliot's famous "objective correlative," or the definition of "diaeresis"? You'll find this an indispensable book, whether you're beginning to research a topic or just flipping through its pages for the enjoyment of dipping into its wealth of entries.

Rich, Adrienne. *What Is Found There: Notebooks on Poetry and Politics*. W. W. Norton, 1993. Rich writes eloquently on language, politics, and poetry's possibilities as an instrument of change.

Rilke, Rainer Maria. *Letters to a Young Poet*. W. W. Norton, 1993. This collection of compassionate, philosophical letters about the creative spirit, written

from the great poet to a young aspiring writer, should be on every poet's
shelf.

Rukeyser, Muriel. *The Life of Poetry*. Paris Press, 1996. This is a timely reprint
of a classic book—first published in 1949—about the role of poetry in our
lives, but as with so much of Rukeyser's work, it is about much more. She
draws on many sources—Native American dream songs, the blues of Ma
Rainey, the science of Darwin and Mead and Einstein—to show us the
multiplicity of experience and that poetry is an index of our deepest fears
and greatest possibilities as a culture. Jane Cooper contributes the foreword.
The Life of Poetry is also excerpted with other works by Rukeyser in *A
Muriel Rukeyser Reader*, edited by Jan Heller Levi, W. W. Norton, 1994.

Steinberg, Sybil. *Writing for Your Life*. Pushcart Press, 1992. *Writing for Your
Life Two*. Pushcart Press, 1995. Interviews with contemporary writers, mostly American, about the art of writing and the job of publishing.

Turco, Lewis. *The New Book of Forms: A Handbook of Poetics*. University Press
of New England, 1986. This small, easy-to-understand book on metrics, son-
ics, and tropes boasts a comprehensive listing and description of over 175
traditional verse forms.

Appendix B:
Anthologies for Further Reading

Algarin, Miguel and Holman, Bob, eds. *Aloud: Voices from the Nuyorican Poets Cafe*. Henry Holt, 1994. Slam-performance–spoken word—cafe poets, in print.

Anzaldua, Gloria and Moraga, Cherrie, eds. *This Bridge Called My Back: Writings by Radical Women of Color*. Second Edition. Kitchen Table: Women of Color Press, 1983. A now-classic collection of nonfiction, fiction, and poetry by feminist women of color, including Genny Lim, Audre Lorde, Pat Parker, and others.

Bruchac, Joseph, ed. *Breaking Silence: An Anthology of Contemporary Asian American Poets*. Greenfield Review Press, 1983. Includes such authors as Marilyn Chin, Jessica Hagedorn, Garrett Hongo, Geraldine Kudaka, Genny Lim, Janice Mirikitani, David Mura, Cathy Song, and Arthur Sze, along with photos and brief biographies and statements by the authors.

Bruchac, Joseph. *Songs from This Earth on Turtle's Back: Contemporary American Indian Poetry*. Greenfield Review Press, 1983. Poems from over fifty Native American writers including Paula Gunn Allen, Diane Glancy, Joy Harjo, Simon Ortiz, and others, along with photos and biographies of the writers. An excellent source for those interested in becoming acquainted with contemporary Native American poetry, especially the early careers of many poets who are now well-known and widely published.

Chester, Laura, ed. *Deep Down: The New Sensual Writing by Women*. Faber and Faber, 1988. One of the first of many collections featuring erotic poetry and prose by women. Includes authors such as Ai, Olga Broumas, Wanda Coleman, Jane Hirshfield, and Sharon Olds.

Codrescu, Andrei. *Up Late: American Poetry Since 1970*. Four Walls Eight Windows, 1989. An "alternative" anthology of experimental work, variously feminist, "language," performance-based, transgressive, subversive, plain-spoken, inscrutable, disjunctive, lyrical, etc. Definitely not the usual suspects. A valuable look at the breadth of current poetic practice.

Dacey, Philip and Jauss, David, eds. *Strong Measures: Contemporary American Poetry in Traditional Forms*. HarperCollins, 1986. A wide range of forms, from acrostics to rubaiyats to villanelles, by writers including John Ashbery, Robert Creeley, Louise Glück, Marilyn Hacker, Donald Justice, Galway

Kinnell, Frank O'Hara, Theodore Roethke, Ellen Bryant Voigt, and many others. Handy indexes at the back: meter and scansion, definitions of all the forms in the book, and further reading on traditional forms and prosody.

DiYanni, Robert, ed. *Modern American Poets: Their Voices and Visions.* Random House, 1987. This book parallels and complements the PBS series, "Voices and Visions," which first aired in 1988 and presents the work and lives of thirteen American poets including Elizabeth Bishop, Robert Frost, Langston Hughes, Sylvia Plath, Wallace Stevens, William Carlos Williams, and others.

Ferguson, Margaret; Salter, Mary Jo; and Stallworthy, Jan. *The Norton Anthology of Poetry.* Fourth Edition. W. W. Norton, 1996. Poetry beginning with "Caedmon's Hymn" and ending with writers born in the fifties. For a closer look at poets from Walt Whitman on, try *The Norton Anthology of Modern Poetry.*

Finch, Annie, ed. *A Formal Feeling Comes: Poems in Form by Contemporary Women.* Story Line Press, 1994. The editor chooses to define formal poetry broadly, including such things as chants and pun-poems as well as the familiar traditional forms like sonnets and villanelles. Each writer is represented with two to six poems, and contributes comments about formal verse.

Forché, Carolyn. *Against Forgetting: Twentieth Century Poetry of Witness.* W. W. Norton, 1993. If you aren't familiar with the stirring, passionate, engaged poetry that the horrors of the twentieth century have brought forth from poets around the world—from the Armenian massacres in the early part of the century to China's Tiananmen Square in 1991—this anthology will prove a stunning introduction to the power and endurance of the poetic voice in any culture and language.

Harper, Michael S. and Walton, Anthony, eds. *Every Shut Eye Ain't Asleep: An Anthology of Poetry by African Americans Since 1945.* Little, Brown, 1994. A strong anthology, eclectic and regionally diverse.

Hirshfield, Jane, ed. *Women in Praise of the Sacred: 43 Centuries of Spiritual Poetry by Women.* HarperCollins, 1994. A comprehensive collection of poems, prayers, and songs that represent the spiritual life of women from the world's earliest identified author (a Sumerian moon priestess) to the women of the first half of the twentieth century. Includes poets as diverse as Makeda, Queen of Sheba, Sappho, Lal Ded, Anne Bradstreet, Emily Bronte, Owl Woman, H. D., Anna Akhmatova, and Sub-ok.

Hongo, Garrett, ed. *The Open Boat: Poems from Asian America.* Anchor Books, 1993. Editor Hongo also contributes an extensive introduction to this collection of contemporary poetry displaying the stylistic, cultural, regional, and ideological diversity among thirty-one Asian-American poets, including Chitra Divakaruni, Li-Young Lee, and David Mura.

Hoover, Paul, ed. *Postmodern American Poetry: A Norton Anthology*. W. W. Norton, 1994. A compilation representing American avant-garde poetry, including the leading Beat and New York-school poets, the projectivists and "deep image" poets, among others. A final section on poetics by poets like Frank O'Hara, Amiri Baraka, and Denise Levertov provides valuable contexts for reading the poems.

Klein, Michael, ed. *Poets for Life: Seventy-Six Poets Respond to AIDS*. Persea Books, 1989. Poets such as Deborah Digges, Mark Doty, Allen Ginsberg, Thom Gunn, Lynda Hull, James Merrill, and others. See also *Things Shaped in Passing: More "Poets for Life" Writing from the AIDS Pandemic*, published by Persea Books in 1997.

Kowit, Steve, ed. *The Maverick Poets*. Gorilla Press, 1988. Presented as an alternative to the more "academic" anthologies used as texts in creative writing programs across the country. In an effort to expand the canon the editor includes many lesser-known poets of the West and says that the common thread they share is a "resistance to the pervasive style of late 20th century verse, with its debilitating preference for the tepid, mannered and opaque." These plain-spoken poets include Alta, Antler, Raymond Carver, Ron Koertge, Jayne Cortez, Harold Norse, Simon Ortiz, Laurie Duesing, Diane DiPrima, and Al Zolynas.

Larkin, Joan and Morse, Carl. *Gay & Lesbian Poetry in Our Time: An Anthology*. St. Martin's Press, 1988. Includes Dorothy Allison, W. H. Auden, James Baldwin, Frank Bidart, Dennis Cooper, Joy Harjo, Tennessee Williams, and many others.

Lehman, David, series ed. *The Best American Poetry*. Simon & Schuster. This highly regarded yearly anthology is edited by a different notable poet each year, who chooses work which first appeared in magazines and contributes an introduction.

Lin, Julia C., trans. *Women of the Red Plain: An Anthology of Contemporary Chinese Women's Poetry*. Penguin Books, 1992. Over one hundred poems by contemporary Chinese women of all ages. Established poets such as Chen Jingrong and Zheng Min, as well as newcomers Shu Ting, Lu Ping, and Li Xiaoyu.

Márquez, Robert, ed. *Latin American Revolutionary Poetry*. Monthly Review Press, 1974. A bilingual anthology of poets from Mexico, Central and South America, and the Caribbean whose poetry speaks against oppression passionately and directly, including Nicolás Guillén, Roque Dalton, Otto René Castillo, Ernesto Cardenal, Iris Zavala, and others.

McClatchy, J. D., ed. *The Vintage Book of Contemporary World Poetry*. Vintage, 1996. Poetry from Europe, the Middle East, Asia, Africa, Latin America, and the Caribbean including Joseph Brodsky, Paul Celan, Nazim Hikmet, Czeslaw Milosz, Octavio Paz, Derek Walcott, and others. Short biographies of poets and selected bibliography. Translations by Elizabeth Bishop, W. S. Merwin, Ted Hughes, Seamus Heaney, and others.

Miller, E. Ethelbert. *In Search of Color Everywhere: A Collection of African-American Poetry*. Stewart, Tabori & Chang, 1994. A beautiful and comprehensive introduction to the history of black American poetry. Poetry from Phillis Wheatley and Jean Toomer to the rap lyrics of Public Enemy and the Black National Anthem. Robert Hayden, Langston Hughes, Lucille Clifton, Bob Kaufman, Maya Angelou, Quincy Troupe, Etheridge Knight, Yusef Komunyakaa, and others.

Milosz, Czeslaw, ed. *A Book of Luminous Things: An International Anthology of Poetry*. Harcourt Brace, 1996. Nobel Laureate Milosz writes in his introduction, "My proposition consists in presenting poems, whether contemporary or a thousand years old, that are, with few exceptions, short, clear, readable . . ." Milosz contributes a brief introductory comment for each poem. Three hundred poems including work by William Blake, Constantinos Cavafy, Zbigniew Herbert, Li Po, Antonio Machado, Charles Simic, and others.

Moffat, Mary Jane, ed. *In the Midst of Winter: Selections from the Literature of Mourning*. Random House, 1982. Moffat compiled this book after the death of her husband; it contains poems and prose from writers of many cultures and historical periods on all the stages of grief. Buson, Catullus, Machado, Olds, Shakespeare, Woolf, and many others.

Peacock, Molly; Paschen, Elise; and Neches, Neil. *Poetry in Motion: 100 Poems from the Subways and Buses*. W. W. Norton, 1996. A collaboration between MTA New York City Transit and the Poetry Society of America, this collects poems and excerpts that have been or will be featured on "Poetry in Motion" placards on public transportation.

Phillips, J. J., ed. *Before Columbus Foundation Poetry Anthology: Selections from the American Book Awards, 1980–1990*. W. W. Norton, 1992. Included are Miguel Algarin, Jimmy Santiago Baca, Amiri Baraka, Juan Felipe Herrera, Wing Tak Lum, Hilton Obenzinger, and many others.

Pond, Lily and Russo, Richard, eds. *Yellow Silk: Erotic Arts and Letters*. Harmony Books, 1990. Poetry and prose selections reprinted from the best of *Yellow Silk*, an erotic magazine that has as its motto "All persuasions, no brutality." Poetry by both men and women including Ivan Arguelles, Marilyn Hacker, D. Nurske, Marge Piercy, Ntozake Shange, and Gary Soto.

Poulin, A., Jr., ed. *Contemporary American Poetry*. Sixth Edition. Houghton Mifflin, 1996. American poets since World War II: John Ashbery, John Berryman, Elizabeth Bishop, Denise Levertov, Charles Olson, Adrienne Rich, and many others. Includes an extensive essay on contemporary poetry, and biographies and bibliographies for the poets.

Rothenberg, Jerome, ed. *Shaking the Pumpkin: Traditional Indian Poetry of the North Americas.* Revised Edition. University of New Mexico Press, 1991. A classic and valuable collection of translations of the traditional poetries of the North American Indians including Seneca, Aztec, Crow, Eskimo, Cherokee, Nez Perce, Zuni, and Papago. Translators include Denise Levertov, Anselm Hollo, W. S. Merwin, Charles Olson, and Edward Field.

Rothenberg, Jerome, ed. *Technicians of the Sacred: A Range of Poetries from Africa, America, Asia and Oceana.* Second Edition. University of California Press, 1985. Prayers, mantras, incantations, hymns, love songs, and chants of native peoples with titles such as "The Abortion" (India: Santal); "A Dispute Over Suicide" (Egypt); and "The Poetics of Hunger" (New Guinea: Trobriand Islands). Includes ancient drawings and descriptions of ceremonial events and rituals with comprehensive commentaries by the editor.

Sturtevant, Jan; Sumrall, Amber Coverdale; and Thornton, Louise. *Touching Fire: Erotic Writings by Women.* Carroll and Graf, 1989. Similar to *Deep Down* and with some crossover, but different enough to stand on its own. Poetry and prose. Poets include Adrienne Rich, Carolyn Forché, Maxine Kumin, Lucille Clifton, and Tess Gallagher.

Wilhelm, James, ed. *Gay and Lesbian Poetry: An Anthology from Sappho to Michelangelo.* Garland, 1995. A historical collection of literature from the ancient Greeks to the Italian Renaissance, arranged chronologically and with commentary about the poets' lives and the context of the work.

Appendix C:
Finding Markets for Your Poems

Poet's Market, Writer's Digest Books, 1507 Dana Avenue, Cincinnati, OH
45207. Published each year, *Poet's Market* contains a huge number of
detailed listings of magazines, chapbook and book publishers, as well as
information on contests, awards, and writers' colonies. Widely available in
bookstores, or order toll-free at 1-800-289-0963.

CLMP Directory of Literary Magazines, Council of Literary Magazines and
Presses, 154 Christopher St., Suite 3C, New York, NY 10014–2839. A less
comprehensive, and therefore maybe less intimidating, listing of literary
journals nationwide, with descriptions of each and a helpful breakdown
state by state.

International Directory of Little Magazines and Small Presses, Dustbooks, P.O.
Box 100, Paradise, CA 95967. Lists some 6,000 book and magazine publishers, including many other genres besides poetry. Editorial descriptions, subject and regional indexing.

Poets & Writers, 72 Spring Street, New York, NY 10012. An important, essential magazine for the national literary community. The classifieds include
calls for manuscripts for magazines, anthologies, chapbooks, and contests.
Listings for grants and awards; articles and interviews.

Poets & Writers also has an Information Center you can call for free from 8
a.m.–noon (eastern standard time), Monday through Friday, which will
answer questions on submitting your work, where to look for publishers'
guidelines for submissions, how to locate a specific literary magazine or
small press, etc.: 1-800-666-2268. See Appendix D for more phone numbers
and e-mail addresses.

Poetry Flash, P.O. Box 4172, Berkeley, CA 94704. Telephone: (510) 525-5476.
A poetry calendar and review for the west, the northwest, and the southwest
that also goes out to subscribers around the world. Lists submission information for magazines, anthologies, and contests. Articles, reviews, interviews,
daily calendar of events, and writers' workshops and conferences.

Appendix D:
More Resources for Writers

Addresses of Other Writers:

The Directory of American Poets and Fiction Writers is published by Poets & Writers biannually and lists the names and addresses of 7,000 writers with a selected list of their publications. Poets & Writers, Inc., 72 Spring Street, New York, NY 10012. Telephone: (212) 226-3586; fax: (212) 226-3963; e-mail: PWSubs@aol.com. For writers published online, try WritersNet, the Internet Directory of Published Writers: http://www.writers.net.

CD-ROMs:

The Norton Poetry Workshop.

Edited by James F. Knapp, University of Pittsburgh. Thirty poems common to *The Norton Anthology of Poetry*, Fourth Edition, and *The Norton Introduction to Poetry*, Sixth Edition, are explored in-depth, and supported by contextual materials such as video, audio, manuscripts, photographs, and paintings. Norton's acclaimed "Essay on Versification" (now interactive) reinforces poetic basics such as scansion, and exercises encourage users to think deeply and connectively about the materials. Poets read and discuss their approach to poetry and talk about their influences and the way historic moments inspired them to, and often necessitated that, they write.

American Poetry: The Nineteenth Century.

Edited by John Hollander and issued by Voyager and The Library of America, this CD-ROM presents 1,000 poems by nearly 150 poets from Philip Freneau through Walt Whitman and Stephen Crane. The work of African-Americans and nineteenth-century translations of traditional Native American texts stand alongside the verse of popular humanists, the lyrics of folk songs, and railroad and outlaw ballads. Supported by audio recordings and photographs.

A Jack Kerouac ROMnibus.

Issued by Penguin USA, this is a multimedia collaboration by fiction writer Ralph Lombreglia, PBS documentarian Kate Bernhardt, and photographer John Smith. The complete text of *The Dharma Bums* with notes, photographs, music, and video is available to users along with selections from other Kerouac texts. A timeline, "Beat family tree," works of art by Kerouac himself, and "A Jack Kerouac Sampler" of nearly thirty minutes of music and readings of Kerouac's work by others.

Poetry In Motion.

Edited by Ron Mann and issued by Voyager. A synergy between the spoken and written word makes this CD-ROM come alive. Twenty-four celebrated poets perform their work to accompany the printed poems: Ntozake Shange, Tom Waits, Gary Snyder, Jayne Cortez, Charles Bukowski, William S. Burroughs, John Cage, Jim Carroll, Miguel Algarin, Amiri Baraka, Ted Berrigan, Robert Creeley, Christopher Dewdney, Diane DiPrima, Kenward Elmslie, Four Horsemen, Allen Ginsberg, John Giorno, Michael McClure, Ted Milton, Michael Ondaatje, Ed Sanders, and Anne Waldman.

Contests, Grants, and Awards for Writers:

Most of the sources listed in this appendix which offer publishing information also include information on various contests, grants, and awards, that range from those for relative beginners to those for well-established writers. PEN (see "Organizations for Poets," below) publishes *Grants and Awards Available to American Writers*. The yearly *Poet's Market* publishes a section on contests and awards; another source is *Poets & Writers* magazine. It's on the Web at http://www.pw.org.

Another online resource is The Writer's Edge, which bills itself as "The Directory for the Writing Community." The Writer's Edge also lists job opportunities, e-zines, writers' conferences, and other valuable information. It can be found at http://www.nashville.net/~edge.

Graduate Programs in Creative Writing:

The Official AWP Guide to Writing Programs is published by Dustbooks, P.O. Box 100, Paradise, CA 95967. Telephone: 1-800-477-6110. This guide describes over three hundred programs in the United States and Canada and is also available through the Associated Writing Programs, or AWP. AWP's address is listed below under "Organizations for Poets." Many graduate programs also have Web sites so you can check out their faculty and course offerings.

Ordering Books by Mail:

The Grolier Poetry Book Shop, 6 Plympton Street, Cambridge, MA 02138. Telephone: (617) 547-4648, or 1-800-234-POEM. This is one of the very few bookstores in the United States devoted exclusively to poetry. Thousands of titles in stock.

Open Books, 2414 N. 45th Street, Seattle, WA 98103. Telephone: (503) 342-3279. Open Books is the only all-poetry bookstore on the West Coast, run by a young mom and pop team. Good, very complete selection.

Spring Church Book Company, P.O. Box 127, Spring Church, PA 15686. Telephone: (412) 354-2359. Toll-free ordering: 1-800-496-1262. Contemporary poetry at a discount. An excellent source for those hard-to-find university and small press titles; they also carry poets on cassette tape, and several anthologies. Call or write for a free catalog.

The Tattered Cover Bookstore, 1628 16th Street, Denver, CO 80202. Telephone: (303) 322-1965. Fax: (303) 629-1704. Toll-free ordering: 1-800-833-9327. One poet we know called this the best independent bookstore in the United States.

Ordering Books Online:

There are many more bookstores online than we could possibly list; here are some of our favorites. As the URLs may change by the time of printing, try a search under the bookstore's title if the information below doesn't get you there.

Amazon.com boasts over 2.5 million—no kidding—titles available. The URL is http://www.amazon.com.

BookPassage in Corte Madera, California, can be e-mailed at bookpass@well.com. It's an independent bookstore which carries a large selection of all kinds of titles, including poetry.

City Lights, the world-famous San Francisco bookstore founded by Peter Martin and Lawrence Ferlinghetti, is on the Web at http://town.hall.org/places/citylights.

Hungry Mind Books, an independent bookstore in Saint Paul, Minnesota, can be found on the Web at http://www.winternet.com/~hungrymi.

Powell's Books in Portland, Oregon, has a Web site where you can place an order, take a look at book reviews, and find links to other bookstores and sites of literary interest. Located at http://www.technical.powells.portland.or.us.

Wordsworth Books in Cambridge, Massachusetts, can be reached through telnet at wordsworth.com, or on the Web at http://www.wordsworth.com. It's a large, general interest discount bookstore.

Organizations for Poets:

These are all fine organizations and deserve your support. As with other online information, URLs may change.

Academy of American Poets, 584 Broadway, Suite 1208, New York, NY 10012–3250. Telephone: (212) 274-0343; fax: (212) 274-9427; e-mail: academy@pipeline.com. The academy, founded in 1934, is the largest organization in the United States dedicated specifically to poetry. It supports programs nationally—readings, events, and prestigious awards and prizes. The academy also can be found on the Web at: http://www.tmn.com/Artswire/poets/academy.html.

Associated Writing Programs, Tallwood House, Mail Stop 1E3, George Mason University, Fairfax, VA 22030. Telephone: (703) 993-4301; fax: (703) 993-4302; e-mail: awp@gmu.edu. AWP is a nonprofit organizaton of writers and creative writing programs. Six times a year it publishes the *AWP Chronicle*, which includes interviews, articles, information on conferences, colonies, and centers, notices of grants and awards, and calls for submissions. In addition to its guide to graduate programs, AWP offers members a *Job List*, listing employment opportunities for writers in higher education, editing, and publishing. The AWP is on the Web at: http://web.gmu.edu/departments/awp.

PEN American Center, 568 Broadway, New York, NY 10012–3225. PEN publishes *Grants and Awards Available to American Writers*, among other services; there is also PEN Center USA West, 672 South Lafayette Park Place, Suite #41, Los Angeles, CA 90057. Telephone: (213) 365-8500. PEN Center USA West offers awards to writers living west of the Mississippi, and grants to western writers with HIV/AIDS.

Poetry Society of America, 15 Gramercy Park, New York, NY 10003. Telephone: (212) 254-9628. PSA is an organization that sponsors events and classes throughout the United States. Three times a year it publishes *PSA News*, with articles, interviews, and reports on PSA events. PSA also sponsors a yearly series of poetry awards. PSA is on the Web at: http://www.poetrysociety.com.

Publishing Online:

There are hundreds of e-zines to submit your work to. We've listed a few in the chapter, "Writing in the Electronic Age"; you'll find the rest listed on the Web itself. Try Yahoo!, the search engine at Stanford, at http://www.yahoo.com/entertainment/magazines/literary/. Be sure to check out the contents of the magazine first, as with print journals; and you'll also want to find out how they prefer submissions—by mail, e-mail, or disk, and whether they accept simultaneous submissions or previously published work.

If you want to publish your own work, start a workshop, or found an e-zine, you'll need to learn the basics of creating a home page. You can find books on Web design at your local bookstore, though the Web itself is the best source of current information. Also, there may be classes on building a Web site available in your area; and a number of Internet service providers now include setup of a personal Web site and maintenance for a monthly fee.

Writers' Colonies:

Artists & Writers Colonies: Retreats, Residences, and Respite for the Creative Mind, by Gail Hellund Bowler, lists nearly 200 colonies in the United States, Canada, and abroad, including detailed information on requirements for application. It is available from Poets & Writers; the address is listed above under "Addresses of Other Writers."

There's also an article on writers' colonies reprinted in *Into Print: Guides to the Writing Life*, also from Poets & Writers. This is a comprehensive collection of the best articles from *Poets & Writers* magazine, updated and revised. It includes articles on topics such as health insurance, libel and permissions, publishing, and many other practical concerns.

Writers' Conferences:

Poets & Writers publishes *Writers Conferences: An Annual Guide to Literary Conferences*. Dates, addresses, fees, deadlines, and workshop leaders; over 200 listings. The address for Poets & Writers is listed above under "Addresses of Other Writers."

Another source of information: *The Guide to Writers' Conferences, Workshops, Seminars, Residencies, Retreats and Organizations*, published by ShawGuides, Inc., 10 West 66th St., Suite 30H, New York, NY 10023, (212) 799-6464.

Many writers' conferences have started Web sites too; try a search using the name of the conference. Two of several currently on the Web are the Bread Loaf Writers' Conference in Vermont (http://www.middlebury.edu/~blwc); and Writers at Work in Utah (http://www.ihi-env.com/w@w.html).

Credits

Index

intimacy, 120, 128
  death and, 42, 43
  family, 30
  sexual, 49, 53

James, Henry, 195
jazz, 143, 156
Jones, Richard, 123–24
journals, 31, 128, 136, 151, 189,
    195–96, 200, 202, 204
  grief, 39
  literary, 61, 196, 205, 206, 211–13,
    217–23
Journals (Plath), 195–96
Jung, Carl, 56, 58

Kenyon, Jane, 58–59, 63, 199
Knight, Etheridge, 156–57, 158
knowing, 19–30
  beliefs and, 243–45
  ideas for writing about, 28–29
Koch, Michael, 129
Kowit, Steve, 173, 244

landscape, 74–76, 80, 98
language, 140
  change and evolution of, 12–13, 142
  displacement of, 48, 53, 111–12
  experiments with, 122, 129–37
  failure of, 71, 116
  figurative, 52, 86, 94–103
  focusing on, 131–33, 173
  graphic, 52–53, 59, 254
  ideas for writing, 135–37
  inflections of, 105–6
  intent and, 133–34
  literal, 94, 96, 99, 122
  modern vs. archaic, 119, 142
  nonlinear, 130, 133–34, 205
  power of, 64–65, 71
  sexual, 46–55
  social and political use of, 64–65
  street, 46
  subversion of, 131, 152
  see also words
"Language of the Brag, The" (Olds),
    234–35

Lee, David, 25
Lee, Li-Young, 33–34
Levertov, Denise, 105, 108–10
Levine, Philip, 34–36, 74, 150
lines, 104–14
  breaking of, 11, 95, 104–12, 113–14,
    115, 121, 129, 189
  control of, 105, 109
  developing of, 163
  end-stopped, 106, 107, 109, 111, 113
  enjambment of, 106–7, 109,
    110–12, 113, 148
  ideas for writing of, 113–14
  length and shape of, 78, 105, 112,
    113, 120, 189
  placement and spacing of, 112, 121
  repetition of, 161–66
  rhythm and, 105–12, 113, 114, 156
  starting of, 112, 121
  tension and relaxation in, 105, 107,
    109, 112, 143
  as units of composition, 104
"Loading a Boar" (Lee), 25
logic, 129
  resistance to, 113, 130–31, 134,
    136–37
"Long Disconsolate Lines" (Cooper),
    153–54
love, 22, 70–71, 120, 198, 254
  falling in, 87–88, 151, 190
  family, 32, 34
  similes and metaphors for, 94, 96,
    150
"Lull, The" (Peacock), 147–48
Lux, Thomas, 163–64

McPherson, Sandra, 104, 157–58
Marlis, Stefanie, 252
memory, 24, 39, 44, 174, 198
  childhood, 72, 74, 75, 77–79, 85,
    165–66, 198
  historical, 67–69, 72
  images and, 85, 86
  painful, 69–71, 99
  of place, 74–76, 79–81
  sensual, 85, 86, 90–91, 92
  sexual, 49–51, 54

About the Authors

DORIANNE LAUX (left) AND KIM ADDONIZIO

KIM ADDONIZIO's first poetry collection, *The Philosopher's Club*, received the 1994 Great Lakes New Writers Award and a Silver Medal from the Commonwealth Club of California. Her most recent collection is *Jimmy & Rita*. A recipient of two fellowships from the National Endowment for the Arts, and a Pushcart Prize, Addonizio has taught at several San Francisco Bay Area colleges. She also offers private workshops.

DORIANNE LAUX is an associate professor of creative writing at the University of Oregon. In his foreword to her first collection, *Awake*, Philip Levine called her poetry "sassy and pugnacious . . . constantly rewarding." Her work has been praised by Adrienne Rich in *Ms* Magazine, and her second collection, *What We Carry*, was a finalist for the National Book Critics Circle Award. Laux has also received a fellowship from the National Endowment for the Arts.